Spiritual Wellness for Life

Inspiring Life Stories of Forgiveness,
Transformation, and Healing

Dolores L. Fazzino, DNP, RN, Nurse Practitioner
Master Energy Healer & Intuitive Counselor

A division of Build.Buzz.Launch.
Media & Publishing

Spiritual Wellness for Life:
Inspiring Life Stories of Forgiveness, Transformation, and Healing
Copyright © 2014 Dolores L. Fazzino, DNP, RN, Nurse Practitioner

Cover design and layout by *SAbER Mountain Design*

Published by BBL Publishing.
Dallas, TX * Oceanside, CA
Printed in USA
First Printing June 2014
ISBN 978-0-9909725-0-1

All rights reserved under the Pan-American and International Copyright Conventions. No part of this book may be reproduced in any form or by any means electronic or mechanical, including photocopying, or by any information storage and retrieval system now known or hereafter invented, without permission in writing from the Publisher.

A division of *Build.Buzz.Launch. Media & Publishing*

www.buildbuzzlaunch.com

This title may be ordered from:

www.SpiritualWellnessforLife.com

Table of Contents

Dedication   7

Introduction   9

Chapter 1   The Initiation   *13*

Chapter 2   Walking between the Worlds (Yes, Helen, there is a Heaven!) *21*

Chapter 3   9/11   *27*

Chapter 4   The Quest: A Little Birdie Told Me   *33*

Chapter 5   Birthing the Soul into Body   *41*

Chapter 6   Forgiveness from Beyond the Veil   *45*

Chapter 7   Experiences from the Casa   *55*

Chapter 8   Our Pets as Familiars   *67*

Chapter 9   My Mother's Transition   *75*

Epilogue   *89*

Illustrations   *93*

About the Author   *103*

Dolores L. Fazzino, DPN, RN

Dedication

I dedicate this book to those who are seekers of truth, and offer hope that there is more than what one can physically see and that we are never alone. In fact, our physical sight is minuscule compared to that of the unseen. As the veils between this world and other dimensions become thinner, the ability to see with our physical eyes will be minor in comparison to what we will see and observe with our spiritual eyes.

I want to acknowledge my family, those who are on earth as well as those who have crossed over. They have provided me with much of the material, experience, and wisdom for this book.

Life has no beginning or ending, as love too is eternal, without ending or beginning.

Dolores L. Fazzino, DPN, RN

Introduction

I realized early on that my life would be different from that of my siblings and school friends. From the day of my dad's healing, my life would never be the same. That event catapulted me on a life-long journey of searching for answers, spiritual and personal growth, and exploring untraditional healing methods.

I knew that more was occurring than what I was taught in school and church. I had witnessed firsthand some rather peculiar things, such as seeing ghosts or dead people and other intangible things. I recall seeing the movie The Sixth Sense with Bruce Willis; when the young boy announced that he could see dead people, I piped up that I could, too! My experiences included a belief in reincarnation; at age four I announced to my mother that I had lived elsewhere before. She played along with me.

Early in my nursing career, l witnessed some odd occurrences within the practice of allopathic medicine. Though these experiences were never talked about openly, these strange phenomena allowed me to know that 1) we are never alone even though we physically think we are, 2) the human soul and spirit can handle much and communicate even though one is comatose, and 3) there is divine intervention.

Throughout my life, both professionally and personally, I have and continue to witness miracles. It is a disservice to humanity to assume that we have it all figured out or that one modality of healing exclusively has the answers.

We are offered many fleeting gifts of hope, inspiration, and love that light the pathways on our earthly journeys. One never knows when or how these gifts come about, yet it is clear that we are never alone. *Spiritual Wellness for Life: Inspirational Life Stories of Forgiveness, Transition, and Healing* is my gift to my earthly brothers and sisters. My intention is to share these stories to assist you, empower you, encourage you, and bring you hope on your earthly sojourns.

I realized early in my life that there was more happening than what I truly could see. It was magical and very as mysterious as well. I have learned to embrace my journey as one that bridges ideas or philosophies. Throughout my career in nursing, I felt my destiny was to bridge the world of allopathic medicine—or western medicine—with complementary and alternative medicine (CAM). This indeed has been so. Yet, there seems to be another bridge that also is occurring, this is the bridging of the spiritual or unseen reality with the physical reality that we see.

I consider my book a coming out party for myself. It is no longer possible to hide behind what truly is my experience in my world.

What we know is that the other dimensions or realms are interconnected. Often we are given fleeting glimpses of these dimensions, so we know that they exist.

As we enter the most powerful time on earth that humanity has witnessed, we are reminded of this interconnectedness and pure love. When the time is right, all will be unfolded. The veils between our world and the other side are lifting and are thinner as connections increase over time. This is especially true as we continue to work on ourselves accepting, respecting, forgiving, and unconditionally loving ourselves; the connections deepen. For true happiness and inner joy is an internal experience that comes from our inner being and not from what is in our external world experience.

Illusions are the external opportunities that provide the most growth in inner strength. Being open and pure in our stance will allow the unraveling of the illusion, often bringing a sense of peace and opportunity for love, acceptance, and compassion.

Our eternal flame, the inner light that radiates from each of our souls, illuminates our way and assists others on their paths as well; it constantly purifies and never diminishes, even though at times one may not feel it, instead feeling disconnected and blind.

It is with heartfelt love and compassion that I share my personal stories, those that have inspired me, moved me, offered hope, and added to my soul's growth. Each story has significant meaning and has provided the most life-changing lessons. We are never alone, though physically we may be by ourselves. It is comforting to know that the spiritual world is there to share information. It is a perfect time in the evolution of humanity to allow the blessings of this divine connection. So may our journey begin . . .

In blessings and inspiration on your earthly journey,

Dolores

Dolores L. Fazzino, DPN, RN

Chapter One
The Initiation

"A true initiation never ends."
Robert Anton Wilson

In 1965 my father threw out his lower back while hitting golf balls with my uncle at the driving range. I was seven years old at the time. My father, a self-employed building contractor, was laid up in bed unable to move due to the pain from the slipped disc in his back. The doctor told us he needed surgery to have the disc removed.

The surgery was successful, but my father's post-operative recovery was anything but successful. He contracted pneumonia and staphylococcus aureus in the hospital and was very ill.

In fact, my father was so seriously ill that he was on his deathbed, and received last rites from our parish priest. As a seven-year-old child I had no idea how serious things were, but I suspected it was really bad.

Although I couldn't know it at the time, this was the beginning of the initiation into my true life. I eventually gained the faith and trust to know that prayers are answered, healings occur, and miracles happen.

At the time, my mother in spite of her overwhelming grief, carried on as if all were well so that my three siblings and I wouldn't be upset.

Her way of coping—emotionless—seemed odd to me. If any of us started to worry or expressed our sadness about our father, we were told not to.

In retrospect, I realize my mother didn't know any other way and was in survival mode; working at home to support the family, caring for four children under the age of seven, and dealing with a seriously ill husband who could die. I cannot imagine the grief, anguish, and fear she was facing. She coped with it the best way that she could. From her perspective, she was trying to protect her children.

My father remained in the hospital for six weeks.

As children we were not allowed to visit the hospital because of the hospital visitation age restrictions at the time.

There was an exception made at Easter. I was so excited; I even made my father an Easter basket I decorated with pastel crayons. It was one of my best pieces of childhood art.

My mom, brother, and I went to my dad's hospital room. Immediately he began to cry. I had never seen my father cry before. He looked horribly emaciated and frail, a fraction of the man I remembered as my father. A man who had stood 5'10" and weighed 175 pounds now weighed 125 pounds and resembled a corpse. My mother, who was on the verge of tears herself, maintained the stoic composure that had allowed her to survive. She told my father that if he was going to act like this, she would not bring us to visit.

For me the cat was out of the bag; I could tell that my father was much sicker than I had been told. It was the beginning of the lesson; I needed to pay attention to my feelings because they are real, even if my mother made less of them. I learned to read between the lines of what my mother was saying or doing and what was really occurring. My life began changing with that understanding.

My father survived. Life at our house eventually returned to normal for us. Several years passed and then the unthinkable occurred.

In the early 1970s, major issues with my father's health developed again. Whenever my father's physical resistance was lowered by a cold or stress, almost spontaneously he would become dangerously ill with an obstruction in his abdomen. He would be hospitalized and would have abdominal surgery to remove these abscesses and allow for continuous drainage from these sites. This occurred not just once but three different times in 1972, 1974, and 1976. Each time a surgery was performed and a six-week hospitalization followed for antibiotics and continuous irrigation and drainage protocols.

This was a very distressing time in my childhood. I was afraid that my father would not come back, that he would die. Once again I wasn't allowed to share my feelings because my mother couldn't handle it. I was fortunate to be able to channel my energy into music. I played the clarinet and received numerous awards in competitions on a state level.

Luckily in 1976, when my father had his last episode, the CT scanner had been developed and was the state of the art diagnostic x-ray machine. The doctors learned that the infections in his abdominal cavity were being seeded from the original surgery site. This information provided a huge breakthrough for the type of treatment my father needed.

The solution to correct this matter was to have a spinal fusion. During the 1970s this surgical procedure was in its infancy in the United States, with many complications including a high risk of paralysis.

During the period that my father had been ill, my mother had been reading extensively about psychic and faith healers as a last resort treatment for him. Though my mother attempted to get my father's consent for this, he did not give it—until he was planning for a high-risk surgical procedure.

While she was at the nurse's station at the hospital she approached the surgeon to ask him about the possibility of getting a faith healer to come in and work with my father. Spirit has an amazing way of intervening. In that moment, the surgeon agreed with my mom that this would be okay. She shared this information with my father who agreed to have a spiritual healer since the surgeon had said that it would be all right to do so.

My mother went back out and told the surgeon that my father had agreed to work with a spiritual healer, and he responded, "A spiritual healer—what are you talking about?" He had no memory of his former agreement.

My father's surgery was scheduled for four weeks later, and in the meantime he was discharged from the hospital. While at home, he received injections of Ancef, a new generation antibiotic to treat staph aureus.

In the meantime, my mother made arrangements to have a minister from Caro, Michigan come to Connecticut. The Reverend Alex Holmes, a Presbyterian minister of the Ministry of Spiritual Healing, had successfully cured his brother of leukemia. He considered himself an instrument of healing from God and in the name of Jesus Christ. He was a last option for many and he said that others came to him after all other traditional means of healing had failed. Reverend Holmes reminded my mother that he was not a Catholic. My mother said that

The Initiation

she believed that there was only one God. With that answer, Reverend Holmes agreed to come and minister to my father. He made it clear that my father should continue to follow medical advice; he worked in tandem with the medical profession.

Reverend Holmes arrived in the middle of January 1976. My parents waited for us to come home from school so that Reverend Holmes could meet us and include us in the ceremony. Both my grandmothers were there, too. Reverend Holmes spoke of passages in the Bible regarding healing and the laying on of hands. Reverend Holmes noticed that my father had a leg-length discrepancy; one leg was longer than the other. We knew about this because my father had worn a lift in his right shoe for years to correct the one-inch variation in his leg lengths. My father was in his slippers, and Reverend Holmes had my father extend his legs in front of him. Reverend Holmes put a book at the bottom of my father's feet and, yes, there was a one-inch difference between the two legs. Reverend Holmes started praying over my father and touching the top of his head and his solar plexus. Not more than five minutes had elapsed when the reverend had my father re-extend his legs; they were equal in length.

There was no possible explanation for this change in the physical world.

My father began to sob spontaneously and uncontrollably, as did the rest of the family. If any of us had doubts that my father could and would be healed, they were dissipated from that moment on. The Reverend continued to pray over my father for another thirty minutes. He then told my father to go and rest.

At the age of seventeen years and speechless with amazement, I had just witnessed a miracle and knew at a core level that my father was going to be fine.

Looking back on it, I can see that this was a major event in my life; one that led me on a journey in which I would question everything I ever learned about healing, western medicine, and how life works on earth. I had witnessed a life-changing event in more respects than I could realize at the time.

Due to the inexplicable nature of the events, my parents warned not to speak of this to anyone. My parents may have felt it wasn't anyone else's business, but I knew that they, like many of their and their parents' generation, were worried about what other people would think. Here I was with this amazing experience—a healing—and I couldn't talk about it. I knew I needed to talk to someone and confided in a friend's parents who were into healing through their religious background. It felt good to finally be able to speak to someone outside of the family and I felt accepted when I shared my experience with them.

Four weeks after this miraculous event occurred, my father's surgeon, on viewing a follow-up CT scan, determined that my father no longer had any evidence of an abnormality in the area of his 1965 back surgery. My father never required back surgery or a spinal fusion. I am pleased to say that my father is still alive and well today, more than thirty years later.

The surgeons were amazed. They considered publishing my father's case in a medical journal. Of course they felt that the antibiotic Ancef caused the miracle, but I know that it was more than that. It was the gift that my father received from a fellow man who was an instrument for healing.

It taught me that we are creators of our own destiny. Opportunities are placed in front of us. It is our free will to grasp and run with them. I am grateful for my mother's insight and persistence in following her intuition when others around her were unable to see the grander picture of what was happening. I learned that what one focuses on manifests in reality. I believe that seeing a miracle allowed me to believe that miracles can and do happen. I also learned the intricate nature of how our thoughts and beliefs create our reality as well. This was the beginning of my life's journey in assisting others with their personal healing.

Furthermore, over the years since this event, I have realized that our deceased relatives assist us from the other side. I believe that my father's father helped with the orchestration of his healing experience, which was my initiation to a different form of healing as well. I know that we are never alone on our journeys and there is always help available. Sometimes we just have to ask. And believe.

What You Can Do to Have Spiritual Wellness

- Know that things in life may not be how they seem. Be curious about life. Information comes from everywhere including the media, books, seminars, and even the National Inquirer.

- Spend some time with children; they are our best teachers. They still have the innocence that gets lost as we experience life here on earth. Children are sensitive and feel things deeply, and are more open and connected to the unseen. Remember the invisible friends you may have had as a child.

- Miracles happen every day! Realize that every day you are alive you are a miracle!

- Angels come in all forms with and without wings.

- Remember to ask for help. The angelic realms and our deceased relatives are eager to help and assist us. However, because we humans have free will on earth, they are not able to intervene unless we ask them. How many times have we realized that we are in a pickle and think that we have to do it alone? Are you one of those lone rangers? If so, open yourself to asking the angels, saints, gurus, ascended masters, as well as your deceased relatives for help. Then watch how your life unfolds.

Chapter Two
Walking between the Worlds, or, Yes, Helen, there is a Heaven!

"The greatest good you can do for another is not just to share your riches but to reveal to him his own."
Benjamin Disraeli

My maternal grandmother Helen was my first spiritual teacher.

Born in the United States in 1901, my grandmother and her family immigrated back to Poland where she was raised. In 1925, my grandmother, her sisters, and mother immigrated back to the United States. She married my grandfather, a man she did not want to marry, in 1931. My grandfather had convinced her to marry him and she did, though her heart was with another man. My grandfather was an abusive man, a man who drank and became violent. Her life with him was not something that she would wish on anyone. My grandfather didn't believe in God or Heaven. Early on in their marriage my grandparents made a pact that whoever died first would come back and tell the other if there was a Heaven.

My grandfather passed on in 1957. My grandmother was relieved that the nightmare was over. About a month after he died, my grandmother shared with me that he had appeared to her in an apparition. She said that he said, "I was wrong. There is a Heaven and it was more than one can expect." With that, he disappeared.

My connection with my grandmother had always been strong and loving. I remember being bonded to her at a very young age. She told me fascinating stories and shared her experiences with metaphysics. I considered her highly intuitive and wise, well ahead of her time, and a very special lady. She taught me about seeing things that other people were not generally aware of. These included spirits, ghosts, or paranormal activity such as pencils moving on the table or pillows falling forward on a couch. My aunts have often said that my grandmother was born at the wrong time. She was an independent, intuitive woman with many gifts that would be appreciated today.

This grandmother was multi-talented—she also taught me how to swear, which did not please my mother at all!

The last year that my grandmother was alive, she lived with my parents at our home in Avon, Connecticut. I was seventeen years old. My grandmother was staying with us not because of health reasons but because the water in her well had frozen over and would not be thawed until the spring. She lived a very simple life. Though she had running water in the house there was an outhouse located in the back yard. There was no heated water, and the stove that warmed the house was fed with coal and wood.

It was fun being with my grandmother; she and I shared a love of animals, especially cats. At that time the family tomcat, Muda, had hooked up with this beautiful petite female black cat. She was tiny—as wide as she was long—and obviously carrying kittens. She was very cute and took a liking to me. She would wait at the bus stop with me and rub around my legs. Little did I know at the time, but our

Muda was bringing this female around our home. It was as if he was bringing her there so that she could be taken care of, a son bringing home his pregnant girlfriend. Quite clever, I thought. So we adopted this beautiful cat and named her Momma.

Momma made herself at home and connected with my grandmother. My grandmother made scrambled eggs for us and for Momma. I recall the day that Momma had her kittens. Grandmother had been watching her as Momma would leave the house, noting where she went and when she came back. The day came that Momma left pregnant and returned no longer pregnant. My grandmother was so excited. She took me to where she had seen Momma come from. We walked over to the property edge where there was a barbed-wire fence. Along the property line was an old hollow tree. In the hollow of the tree we heard the whimpering mews of newborn kittens. Momma was also there. My grandmother said it was okay to put my hand in there since the cat really trusted me and had a connection with me.

I placed my hand in the hollow and felt the softness of Momma and several smaller fur balls. Excitedly I reached in and removed the kittens one by one. They were incredibly beautiful, smaller than the palm of my hand and with their eyes closed. I remember the feeling of being able to see new life and to have the complete trust of an animal. There were five kittens in the end. Each was as unique as a sunset in color and temperament.

My grandmother and I returned to the house with the kittens and Momma. We told Momma, "Good work!" It was a special moment that I shared with my grandmother, one that I still cherish to this day.

Easter came early that year, at the beginning of April. I remember overhearing both grandmothers speaking to each other while I was in the other room. I overheard my Grandma Helen, the grandmother I was close to, say that she was not going to be around much longer. I went outside and started to cry. I felt sadness and an empty feeling of loss inside of me. I thought, "Why is she talking this way? What does this mean?" Intuitively I felt she was right and that really scared me.

Three weeks passed. During that time, grandmother shared a dream with my mother and me. She had dreamt of her husband, my grandfather, who had been deceased for about twenty years. She said he was on a ladder next to a house. She asked him what he was doing; he replied that he was building houses. She asked him where, and he said she would not like where the houses were. This really disturbed grandmother, since she did not want to be buried next to her husband when she passed away, yet this could very well be a possibility.

The time came for my grandmother to return to her farm home in the country. The water pump was fixed and in operating order. The evening of her departure, I remember giving her a hug and kiss goodbye. As I held her, I started crying. I had an awful feeling I would never see her again. I was on my way to work and my mother asked me why I was crying. I told her of my fear.

That evening my mother took my grandmother home, settled her in, washed her floor, and left to come back to our home. The next morning my parents received a phone call from the operator. The operator connected my mother and my grandmother. Grandmother said she hurt all over and could not see. The operator dispatched an ambulance to my grandmother's and my mother called an aunt who lived nearby. My aunt arrived as the ambulance got there. Apparently my grandmother had gotten up, felt terrible pain in her body, collapsed, and lost her sight. The ambulance rushed her to the hospital and my mother rushed to the hospital to meet her there.

Unfortunately, my grandmother did not make it to the hospital and passed away in the ambulance. I was in a Saturday reading class when this happened. At the end of class my Aunt Sara and my Grandma Carmella met me, both in tears. I knew that Grandma Helen didn't make it.

This was my first experience with the death of someone close. I didn't understand how someone could be here one moment and gone the next. What was I going to do without my Grandma?

In preparation for my grandmother's funeral, my mother and her siblings decided to have my grandfather's coffin moved to where my grandmother would be buried. My mother said that she had been thinking about this a long time prior to my grandmother's sharing her dream. I felt my grandmother didn't want to be buried next to my grandfather, possibly because of their abusive marriage. But my mother and her siblings decided to have my grandfather's body exhumed and buried next to my grandmother.

For several months after my grandmother's passing, I was very worried and concerned. I remember one evening being home by myself in my room listening to music. I was thinking about my grandmother and wondering about her. The next thing I knew, there she was, materialized in front of me! She was as real as if I were standing next to her. She was dressed in the gown that she was buried in, a dress that I had made for her for to wear to a cousin's wedding.

She said to me in her broken English with her strong Polish accent that she was fine. She wanted to come back to me to tell me that everything was going to be okay. I was able to give her a hug. I felt a deep connection with her and an extreme sense of peace, and truly felt that I was going to be fine as well.

Luckily for me, my parents did not think that I had lost my mind and rather used the information as a healing for them as well. My parents felt serenity and peace; they also witnessed paranormal activity—pictures on the wall moving or pillows on the couch flipping over. They would telepathically ask who was there and the answer would come back as "Mom."

What You Can Do to Have Spiritual Wellness

- When you think of a deceased family member or friend or pet, know that they are very much around you and are thinking of you as well. Pay attention to these thoughts, they may be telepathically trying to communicate with you.

- If you see something such as things moving without someone physically there moving the item, be curious, and do not be afraid. Ask in your mind, or telepathically, who is there. The first answer that pops into your mind is usually who it is. Try not to analyze it and figure it out. Just take the information. If you start analyzing, you disconnect from the flow of information.

- Pay attention to your dreams. If you remember your dreams keep a journal by your bedside to record them. If you do not remember your dreams, prior to going to bed, ask in a prayer or meditation that you remember your dreams when you awake in the morning.

Chapter Three
9/11

"Act as if what you do makes a difference. It does."
William James

Over time, humanity has gone through many massive growth opportunities. These include natural disasters such as plagues, floods, droughts, earthquake, tsunamis, erupting volcanoes, and tornados to name a few, and man-made disasters such as war, holocaust, imprisonment, and terrorist activity.

During these times of major strife that lead to hopelessness, there is a shining light of hope. This hope manifests in masses of humanity coming together to aid each other during our most challenging times. It is unfortunate that it takes something of a great magnitude to create a shift in people's consciousness, to wake people up!

It is human nature to react to circumstances, to give assistance, and to want to make things better. Over the years, I have moved from my young understanding of the presence of invisible forces to a belief that sometimes humanity makes great sacrifices to advance civilization. There really are no mistakes, only lessons. Even though many lives may be lost, the souls who perished in these disasters, both natural and man-made, were active participants, and, in fact, this experience may have been part of their karma, to assist in the advancement of humanity. This idea eliminates the need for blame and judgment of others. However, our egos are bent on making someone pay for our difficulties, even though they are assisting in the advancement of humanity. Each of us is connected to one another and human suffering affects us all. There is no way that it cannot do so.

The terrorist attacks on the United States, September 11, 2001, are an example of this. The events of that day have completely changed life for many on multiple levels. I believe that something of this magnitude had to occur to allow for a shift in consciousness. The souls that were lost in this tragedy were there on purpose, whether or not they remember planning this prior to this incarnation. They are true warriors assisting in the evolution of spirituality. It is with deepest and sincerest gratitude and humility that I recognize these souls.

At the time, the events of 9/11 were raw and very real for me. For the next two weeks, I lived in a fog, asking, "Did this really happen? Was it just a dream? A really bad nightmare?" I recall that no one could believe that this had occurred, let alone in the United States. Everyone seemed paralyzed. We all witnessed the entire country's belief system come to a complete stop in a matter of minutes. There was much tension, fear, and worry.

How could this possibly have happened here in our country, and what would happen next? Many thought this should be happening in someone else's back yard, not ours. The reality was that it was happening here, and that no one was exempt from the effects of mass destruction.

Everything became frightening.

Two weeks later, on September 29, 2001, I was in Northern California at a ranch in Lake County. I was going to surprise my sister Linda, who was there from the east coast on a retreat. I flew up from San Diego for the weekend. It was great to reconnect with her, especially since I surprised her.

At the ranch there is a labyrinth, which is a large walking meditation grid. This particular one was constructed outdoors.

There are several different types of labyrinths, this one in particular was a replica of the nave floor of the Notre Dame de Chartes outside of Paris. That labyrinth is considered sacred geometry and was constructed about 1201 AD.

The Chartes Labyrinth is a series of eleven convoluted pathways around a flower-shaped center known as the Rose. These pathways are symbolic, possibly similar to the human brain's pathways. In the Chartres Cathedral, the rose at the center is a reflection from a stained-glass window. It is symbolic of enlightenment; its Eastern equivalent is the lotus. The six petals of the rose signify the six days of creation or the six levels of evolution in Christian theology—mineral, plant, animal, human, angelic, and divine.

The purpose of the labyrinth is to bring us closer to our core as we walk the pathway, a metaphor of one's life journey. The path assists walkers to circle inward toward the center of their soul. Once at the center one moves towards a goal (a petal on the Rose) allowing one to release emotions that have been carried within in order to create or envision a solution as one turns around and works his or her way back to the outside or beginning of the labyrinth. It is a left-brain to right-brain process or a shift that occurs when one walks the path.

I began my walking journey after reciting an invocation. On my journey I felt a presence with me. It was a strange yet familiar feeling. The essence of my kind grandfather, who had passed on when I was four years old, was present. The warmth I felt was comforting. My grandfather's energy had come to me before in my past when major spiritual experiences or initiations had occurred in my life. Because of those prior experiences, I was alerted that something big was about to happen and trusted and accepted that.

I continued on my walk. As I approached the center rose, I was drawn to the areas of the rose that symbolized the human and the angelic. As I reached the rose petal for angelic, I immediately felt something pulling at my crown chakra attempting to bring my attention somewhere else. I immediately centered and grounded myself in my body and then let part of my consciousness leave my body to journey three thousand miles away to the remains of the World Trade Center. I was quietly awed as I became conscious that I was in two different places, miles apart and fully present in both simultaneously. I experienced an overwhelming feeling of sadness. Tears flowed from my eyes effortlessly.

To be present in spirit at the World Trade Center and feel the devastation and loss of life that had occurred was so horrific that I was nearly inconsolable. The energy from this event was still very much present. I sensed that because this event occurred so quickly and suddenly there was much chaos in the unseen dimension as so many souls and spirits were crossing over at once, and that a few had not yet made that transition to their home. These souls were lost in transition, so to speak, because of the confusion.

There were three souls who were lined up looking at me. As I gazed into each of their eyes, I felt these spirits were having difficulties crossing over to the other side.

The first spirit was a tall man with light brown hair, a well-groomed professional, probably about the age of thirty-four. He told me that he was concerned about his family and could not leave them. He had young children at home and was worried about them. I reassured him and told him that his family would be cared for and that they would be all right. He said thank you and moved onto the white light.

The second young man was about twenty-seven; he had darker hair and was a little shorter. He said to me, "Teach me how to fly, I forgot how to." The tears were continuously pouring down my face, as they are now as I reflect back and write. I guided him through this process and he flew off into the white light.

Lastly, a beautiful young woman about the age of twenty-three appeared in front of me. She had the most stunning long black curly hair, delicate face and eyes. She also asked me to teach her how to fly, because she did not know how. So I instructed her and she moved toward the white light.

This entire experience took me aback. In that moment I realized that there was more to my mission on this earth than I had imagined. I was honored to be of service to these souls to assist them back home.

My awareness then shifted back to where my physical body was in Northern California at the labyrinth; I continued out of the labyrinth. At the end of my journey, I turned around to say a prayer of thanks and saw three butterflies flying together off into the sky. According to Native American totem symbology, butterflies are symbolic of transformation, metamorphosis, and the courage to change. I had witnessed three souls being transformed as they crossed over to the light.

What You Can Do to Have Spiritual Wellness

- Pay attention and give yourself permission to observe nature, better yet spend more time outdoors in nature. Our animals, insects, birds, reptiles, fauna, and flora all have messages for you. When one of nature's creatures crosses your path, consider looking up its meaning in a book on animal totems, or on an internet website on animal totems. Explore and reflect on the meaning and message you are given from that particular creature.

- Give yourself permission to daydream and reflect. This allows your inner wisdom to assist you in creating and building your reality. Things happen in dream form first before they manifest in reality.

- Know that everything is connected. Life is a matrix involving many dimensions or levels.

- Life continues after death; it just changes form. The soul or the person is housed in a physical body. When the body dies, the soul is released from the body into a new form often invisible to the human eye, yet ever present and alive.

- Look for and be open to synchronicities in your life. Life is a synchronicity, a coming together of people, places, and things that occur almost magically.

Chapter Four
A Quest: A Little Birdie Told Me

*"To do more for the world than
the world does for you—that is success."*
Henry Ford (1863-1947)

Fall is fire season in San Diego County. In the fall of 2003, the San Diego wild fires destroyed hundreds of thousands of acres and well over two thousand homes. Listening to the news and sensing the general human reaction, allowed me to see that this was indeed a time for nature's purification. Fire is a natural cleanser and purifying agent. When energy is stagnate and needs to be changed, fire comes to assist in the transformation of what is stagnate and stuck.

I find it puzzling when an area is hit with fire that one or two homes may be spared from burning, yet the surrounding houses are burnt to the ground. It's as if the fire has its own consciousness and knows where it needs to go.

Along with the material losses that many people had incurred, there were some who experienced the loss of family. This story is about a family who not only lost their home, but their sixteen-year-old daughter Ashleigh, who perished in the fire. Some family members escaped with minor injuries but Ashleigh's older sister, Allyson, ended up at the UCSD burn unit with second and third degree burns over 85% of her body. I knew very little about the Roach family until I had the honor of visiting with Allyson and her family at the hospital.

Upon arriving back in San Diego from a week in Orlando, Florida, I was awakened on Sunday, October 26 by a bird tapping at my bedroom window. I ignored the bird, but it remained persistent with its tapping. This continued to occur every morning until November 1.

On October 28, I was reading about a memorial service for the daughter of a colleague who was the evening nursing supervisor at Palomar Medical Center. Clutching my chest I could feel the pain and loss that this family was experiencing. I started asking questions.

I did not realize the significance of the message I was receiving from the bird tapping at my bedroom window until October 31. On October 30, I was assisting a colleague of mine, Dr. Yale Kadesky, a plastic surgeon at Palomar Medical Center, during a surgical procedure. Both Yale and I would often discuss alternative and complementary medicine, as well as my interests in mediums and medical intuition during our surgical procedures. We conversed about the recent tragedy that had occurred with the wild fires in San Diego. Laurie Roach, a nursing supervisor at Palomar Medical Center, and her family had experienced the loss of her sixteen-year old daughter Ashleigh, and her oldest daughter Allyson, 20 years of age, was on life support in the burn unit at UCSD Medical Center in San Diego.

Yale informed me that he had been asked by Laurie Roach to be a consultant on Allyson's case. He shared information with me about the family and Allyson's prognosis. I asked him if he would like me to go with him to support him, as well as to provide assistance to the family. He enthusiastically replied, "Yes." I agreed to accompany him and said that I wanted to meet first with the family, to introduce myself and to share my gifts with them, and receive their consent to visit with their daughter Allyson.

I realized that everything was beginning into fall into place, and understood what my role was in this story. That morning I remember asking the bird who was tapping at my window, "What is it you are trying to tell me? You have seed in your feeder and water in your fountain." I realized that the bird was trying to tell me something. As the pieces of the puzzle were coming together, I began to feel that it had something to do with the Roach family.

The next day, October 31, at the UCSD burn unit, I met with Yale and the Roach family. I had the privilege of spending some time with them in the waiting area outside the burn unit.

I felt an immediate connection with Laurie Roach. I told Laurie and her husband John what I do. I told them that I am a nurse practitioner, an energy worker, and a spiritual medium. I explained that I am able to connect with the other side and that I also worked with her mother at Palomar Medical Center.

I asked her what significance birds might have with her daughters. She immediately spoke about her daughters having a way with animals especially Ashleigh, who had perished in the fire. Laurie recalled that a few days prior to the fires, a neighbor's pet bird, a cockatiel had flown onto their roof and Ashleigh had climbed a ladder and the bird came to her, a stranger, and that she returned it to its owner. Laurie described Ashleigh as the Pied Piper of animals; they were always around her and drawn to her.

After this information was shared with me I realized that I had been receiving a spiritual message from the bird that had been tapping at my bedroom window all week, and recounted that experience to Laurie. I also explained to the Roach's that often times souls are in a state of indecision about whether they want to stay or leave the earth plane, especially when a physical trauma, emotional trauma, or tragedy occurs and they are in a coma-like state. The decision is the soul's choice. The soul makes the decision freely whether to stay or to move onto the next dimension. Through prayer and communication with the soul, we can empower them and support them in their decisions.

I was granted permission to visit Allyson in the burn unit. Her father, John, escorted me in. He clutched my hand in his tightly. I sensed his need to hold it together for the support of his family. I sensed his strength and courage being there for them even though he was on the verge of his own overwhelming grief. I offered support to him, asking how he was doing and let him know that no matter what happens she will be all right.

As we approached Allyson's room, I was appreciative of the entire situation and of creation. I perceived a lightness and brightness to the room that was not from electrical lights but of a spiritual light.

Allyson was lying in her bed, bandaged from head to toe, on a ventilator, and in a coma-like state. Deep sedation places the patient in a drug-induced coma-like state. This is done to allow for better pain management for the patient and it allows the body to rest.

I introduced myself to Allyson, as if she was totally present even though she was in an altered state. I explained to John that even though she was in a coma-like state she was very much present in the room. John added that I was a family friend who was here to help her get better. I told Allyson that I would be touching her feet. This was the only area that we were allowed to touch, due to extent of her burns, but is also the area where I usually do my work.

Immediately, as I tapped into her energy I felt a burning inside my chest. While this was happening, the nurse in the room told me that Allyson had severe inhalation burns inside her lungs; because of this, the physicians would do a daily procedure to remove the dead tissue to avoid a potential infection or pneumonia from occurring. They did this under heavy sedation. I asked the nurse whether they were sure that she was getting adequate levels of sedation since I was feeling Allyson's pain in my body. The nurse replied that it is difficult to know since the patient is unresponsive verbally. As a nurse myself, I know that even though the patient is comatose it does not mean that there is not physical pain that they could be experiencing.

Next, I encouraged John to continue to talk with Allyson. He told her that both he and her mom were going to dinner with close family friends and that they were going to recall some funny stories from their shared past.

Immediately, I felt an overwhelming need to say, "Remember the dangling carrot and horse story," and I did so. Surprised, John said, "Oh, my gosh, that is Ashleigh." Ashleigh was the daughter who perished in the fire!

I continued to tap into the energy; I was then taken to an area in the room where three spirits /souls were present. A young girl with dark long hair told me she was Ashleigh, an older woman (someone who could be a grandmother figure), and the spirit of Allyson, who was in the hospital bed in a coma. Even though I did not feel that the older woman was directly related to Ashleigh and Allyson, I felt that they were connected in some way. The older woman was a little taller than

Ashleigh, with grayish short hair, on the chubby side and full of life. Ashleigh was holding a black and white cat.

I tapped into them; Allyson was with them, yet she was not sure whether to stay there with the two or to go back to her body. I spoke to her telepathically. I told Allyson's spirit that it was her choice whether or not she wanted to stay. And that whatever choice she made we would support her in that decision. In addition, I said that there are many, many people who she knows and many she has not yet met that want her to stay, if she would please take that into consideration as she makes her decision. She told me that she would consider that.

It was a moving experience to see these three spirits together, two of which were deceased and one in indecision. It was verification for me that we are all connected even though physically this cannot be seen.

I asked if there was anything further that needed to be addressed or discussed. They said no. I thanked the three for their willingness to be there to communicate with me and that I would continue to hold the light for them.

As I left Allyson's room I felt completeness. I walked back to the waiting area and met up with the Roaches, Yale, and a couple who were neighbors of the Roach's. I shared with them what I had experienced. I told them about a funny story that Ashleigh mentioned—the horse and the dangling carrot. Interestingly this particular story involved the neighbors that were standing with the Roaches.

The neighbors said that the girls used to come over to their corral where they kept their horses and feed them carrots that they had planted in the garden adjacent to the corral, thus the dangling carrot.

I asked the family about the three spirits that were present in

Allyson's room. The older woman was a very close family friend who had passed earlier. The family told me that Ashleigh passed away on this woman's birthday. The cat that Ashleigh was holding was her favorite pet that also had previously passed away. I shared with the Roaches that Allyson was there with these spirits and was not sure whether or not she wanted to stay or go. The two deceased in spirit were together with Allyson staying close. I told the parents what I received and the conversation that I had with her.

I thanked them for allowing me to be of service to Allyson and their family. I felt that comfort was brought to them on numerous levels. And do you know the amazing thing is that bird stopped tapping at my window after that!

Allyson has made a full recovery, is married, and a mother of one.

What You Can Do to Have Spiritual Wellness

- Connect with nature, there are messages for you. It may be an animal, insect, or other creature of nature that has crossed your path.

- Know that those in a coma or altered state are still very much present. The soul or spirit is very close to the physical body, and can hear you, and even communicate with you as well.

- Consider embracing your sensitive side. Give yourself permission to experience all your feelings, including the ones that make you uncomfortable.

- Open your heart and allow it to stay open no matter what is happening in your life.

Dolores L. Fazzino, DPN, RN

Chapter Five
Birthing the Soul into Body

*"Souls are poured from one into another
of different kinds of bodies of the world."
Jesus Christ in Gnostic Gospels: Pistis Sophia*

Much has been shared about those crossing over, experiencing transition to eternal life. Very little is written about what actually occurs as the soul enters the body at birth. There are many ways this may occur.

Places of birthing and death, such as hospitals, are portals or openings between the earth and the other side. Souls enter and souls leave. These are the crossroads where transitions are made. Being involved with hospitals for most of my career as a nurse, I have witnessed many births as well as deaths.

What I have experienced is that in the birthing suites there is a magnitude of white light that continually pours from the heavens into these areas, so as to provide a path for the incoming soul to be guided towards their new bodies. The Guardian Angels assist in this process. No matter what type of birth, vaginal or Cesarean section, the team of angelic beings and light spirits is there to assist the soul and escort it and assist with its integration in its new physical home for this earthly incarnation and journey.

All births are different. All souls are different. All life journeys are different. This may be so because of karmic conditions, or what the soul needs in order grow and advance at a deep level.

The soul's journey begins prior to the process of birth and with the physical birthing the soul is handed off to the parents. The soul prior to the birth may be intermittently in the new physical body while in the mother's womb or off gathering further wisdom and information prior to actual physical birth. Sometimes the soul is physically grounded and integrated in the new body at birth or sometimes the integration may occur several hours after the physical birth of the body.

The story that I am sharing is about the birthing of my close friend's second daughter.

My longtime friends, the Herberts, asked me to stay with Judy after she delivered her second child in the hospital. The birth of Courtney Herbert was a normal uncomplicated delivery. She was born at 4:50 p.m. on February 4, 2003. The caring nursing staff, physicians, extended family members and her parents, John and Judy, surrounded her.

Judy was scheduled for a tubal ligation, a separate sterilization procedure, after the delivery of Courtney. Because of this, Judy had not had the time to truly connect and bond with her newborn daughter Courtney. About 8 p.m. Judy was returned to her room following her procedure. She was greeted by a gathering of extended family members, immediate family, and friends. Judy's eldest daughter, Calista, age two years and four months, was very distraught to see a new baby in her mother's arms.

I immediately had a flashback to my childhood. I was the same exact age as Calista when my newborn sister had been born. I had been feeling somewhat lost and felt that my whole world had been turned upside down.

Trying to comfort Calista was difficult, for she seemed totally inconsolable. About 8:30 that evening, all the family and visitors had left. The plan was that I would stay with Judy overnight to assist her with Courtney, and Judy's husband would go home to tend to Calista.

Both mother and new daughter were spending some quiet time together when a beautiful white light appeared on the ceiling. This light flowed down upon the baby and surrounded both the baby and mother, who was looking at the baby.

In that moment I was shown the gift of the soul bonding into the physical being or vessel—the newborn, and the bonding between that returning soul and the mother. There was a beautiful peacefulness, a serenity that overcame the room and lingered for a while.

It was a true gift from heaven. "So that's how the soul enters the physical body!" I thought to myself.

During the night, newborn Courtney was very colicky and she cried inconsolably. It was interesting to note that once the spirit or soul of the newborn engaged with the physical body, it was readjusting itself to the confines of a relatively small form. Imagine a spirit or soul being everywhere, not in a body, free-floating and ever expanding, and then being funneled into a small container. It makes sense that it would be rather uncomfortable.

What a blessing it was for me to witness a birth, from the physical perspective as well as from the spiritual.

What You Can Do to Have Spiritual Wellness

- Witness the birth of a child or animal; it will change your life.

- If you are surrounded by a lot of death and loss, surround yourself with events of birth and growth as well.

- Connect with nature and experience the seasons.

- Give yourself permission to live your life differently. Be like a caterpillar that changes and morphs itself into a butterfly.

- Accept that change is the only constant in life. Know that we are forever changing, growing, and transforming ourselves, and that birth and death are normal processes in the evolution of life and events.

Chapter Six
Forgiveness from Across the Veil

"Unforgiveness is like drinking poison and hoping the other person dies."
Margaret Stunt

Forgiveness is a sensitive topic and a process that seems to raise emotions for many individuals. For some people, forgiving others is an uncomfortable task. It seems easier to hang onto the resentments and hurts as if they were our battle trophies. "They did me wrong and they are going to pay for it," or "I have to be right no matter what the cost." And that cost can be robbing us of our joy, love, health, or a plethora of other opportunities. These resentments or acts of unforgiveness are what keep us in the karma loop.

The purpose of forgiveness is to release the anger and resentment and let go of our ego. It is liberating, and allows us to move on. Remember, the act of forgiveness is not forgetting what happened. It is not continuing the experience of a physical and or emotional charge or reaction regarding the issue requiring forgiveness. It is learning the lesson without attachment and coming to peace with neutrality and acceptance.

What I have learned is that forgiveness as well as love knows no boundaries. Karma exists due to a lack of willingness to forgive. So we continue to reincarnate to work through our karma and continue to learn those life lessons that will allow us to grow at soul level.

I view forgiveness as a simple process. We as humans involve our ego, and make it much more complicated than it should be. One of our human flaws is that if it is not complicated, it will not work. Often we are hanging onto resentments that have become such a part of who we are, that they continue to drive us automatically. These unconscious resentments are the ones that give us the "aha" moments when we cross over to the other side and have our life review.

My process is simple. Just ask God or Source or with whomever you have a connection, to assist you with forgiveness work, especially for things that you do not remember that you have done. Then say, "I ask forgiveness for things that I have done to others, consciously or unconsciously. I ask forgiveness of others, whom I may have hurt either consciously or unconsciously. And lastly, I ask forgiveness for myself, since I am the hardest on myself."

For those on the cusp of making their transition to the other side, forgiveness is helpful in order to lighten the emotional or mental baggage that may prolong the process of death. In my experience, working with forgiveness and the previously mentioned process assists those to make a smoother transition with grace.

As part of the ascension process that beings on earth and humanity is experiencing, many opportunities to heal the past and unload emotional, mental, physical, as well as spiritual baggage—or karma-bearing situations and circumstances—are available to us. Much of the karma that we carry from lifetime to lifetime is due to acts of non-forgiveness. There may be situations where we have been holding onto grudges, or we may not have been aware of how our behaviors had an effect on those around us. Mostly it is the ego that is hanging onto being right no matter what the cost. I am sure we all can relate to this!

If we look at the concept of time, it only exists on earth. There is no such thing as time in the spirit realm. Time also is malleable and can be sped up or slowed down. Have you noticed how the years seem to be going faster, and it is not because we are aging? Or that there never seems to be enough time in our day? It's as if we are now living in sixteen-hour days instead of twenty-four hour days. Thus the speeding up of time called the collapsing of time is proven in quantum physics.

Because of this, accessing other lifetimes and dimensions is easier. So working through a karmic condition is more rapid, easier, and effortless. All parties, including those who are alive and those who are deceased, have the ability to connect with each other and work through unresolved issues that are preventing any party from moving forward on their soul-growth path and evolution.

Today it is not unusual to work through issues that are in need of forgiveness from either side of the veil. Recently, as an energy healer and medium, I have found forgiveness being a theme and common thread for many of my private clients. What I mean by medium, is the ability to work with both the spiritual world and the physical world to assist in one's healing through interventions in a person's energy field. This is done by seeing the energetic patterning of thoughts, beliefs, and how they are connected in the physical body as blockages or diseases. Or by seeing how these blockages prevent us from moving forward in our lives and keep us stuck. Sometimes it's the things that we are not conscious of that are still in our energy field. The following story is from my personal experience.

My paternal grandmother passed away September of 1988. She lived to age eighty-eight and her name was Carmella. Carmella was a traditional Sicilian woman who immigrated to America from the old country in 1913. Her life prior to her immigration to America was difficult. Shortly after she came to America at the age of sixteen, she married my grandfather, Salvatore. Their life together consisted of raising eight children, surviving the Great Depression, several wars, and losing the family farm. My grandfather passed away suddenly at age sixty-three from a heart attack. From that day on my grandmother wore the traditional black mourning costume of the Sicilian widow.

With my grandfather's passing my grandmother had an underlying sadness about her. As a child I recall her being rather scary in that black outfit. I felt that her energy was a bit off as well. She was often sad, and always talked about wanting to die. She had a tendency to be very domineering, and mean as well. She definitely had her favorite children; if you were one of them you were a chosen one.

One time when she came to visit my father when he was ill, I recall telling her that I did not like her. She was always so negative and sad, and wearing that black outfit she scared me as well. I could feel that she was draining my energy. I told her that I hated her. My parents punished me for being disrespectful. I was five years old and was only speaking my truth. I was told that I was to like her because she was my grandmother.

Although my grandmother had eight live children, she had her favorites. My grandmother was fond of my father and my uncle Jim; however, no matter what my father did, it seemed that it was never good enough. It seemed a bit twisted and really did not make much sense to me. Being the obedient daughter, I did as my parents told me, and went out of my way to get to know my grandmother.

My grandmother would always say that she wanted to die; I could sense that she felt a void within herself. As I got to know her more, I found her to be a kind yet sad person, not happy with herself, her accomplishments, or her life. Our relationship would have its moments, yet I was a devoted granddaughter and looked after her.

At that time, however, I had limited knowledge of what boundaries were and their importance to those who are sensitive to other people's energy fields. I recall visiting my grandmother as an adult and feeling extremely tired after our visits together. This would happen often. I found what was even worse was that if I visited her when I was feeling blue or depressed myself, I felt absolutely terrible when I left her house.

I realized that my grandmother was unconsciously tapping into my energy field to fill hers up, this is called psychic vampirism. Interestingly, my father had had similar experiences when he visited her also. Because I was not aware of what was happening at the time this occurred, I felt extremely drained and more depressed than ever.

My grandmother was self-contained and independent until her eighty-sixth birthday. Her eldest son Jim had recently passed away suddenly in his sleep from a heart attack. She was inconsolable, and within the next six months fell into a deep state of depression. She lost her will to live, was severely depressed, and suffered from insomnia. She had a lack of appetite not just for food, but for life itself. She really wanted to die. She never seemed to recover from this loss. I found it distressing that she carried on this way and was unable to see the larger picture. She had seven other children who were alive and well, and numerous grandchildren who were alive and who she could have enjoyed.

Shortly after her birthday, Carmella moved in with my parents; she required continuous supervision. She was angry, defiant, and it became apparent that she had been holding grudges for decades against other family members and people that she knew. It surprised me that she was still speaking of events that had occurred over eighty years ago and was still very angry and resentful over these situations.

By the spring of 1988, my grandmother was placed in a convalescent home. She continued to be sad and withdrawn; she truly had lost all will to live.

She passed away in September 1988, at the age of eighty-eight. I did not attend her funeral since I had recently relocated from Connecticut to the West Coast in San Diego.

I recall the time around her passing. I had moved into my new home and was living by myself. I had a bookshelf in my home, which was situated where no wind or breeze could disturb it. On this bookshelf I had unframed photographs that were propped up against various curios that were on the shelf. Several days prior to my grandmother's passing, I found the pictures face down on the bookshelf. Not thinking much of this, I repositioned the photos again.

The next, day my keys that had been in my purse were on the kitchen table. They started to jingle by themselves. Again, I was by myself and there was no other being or animal that I could physically see. That evening, I threw a piece of rolled paper into the trashcan in the kitchen. The trashcan was half full. The piece of paper projected itself out of the trashcan and rolled across the floor. These events continued for two days; I then received a phone call from my parents informing me that my grandmother had passed away. At that moment I realized that the poltergeist events that I had been experiencing were signals from my grandmother's soul who was attempting to get my attention.

After I finished speaking with my mother, I closed my eyes and spoke to my grandmother telepathically. I told her that this is what she had always wanted, to be dead, so she should now go to the white light in peace. All the non-physical activity ceased in my home.

It was not until eight years later that I had the most healing experience to date. It was in 1996 and I was on my daily walk through Torrey Pines State Reserve in San Diego. As I was walking a trail, I felt a presence with me. I turned around, yet no one was there. I continued to walk towards a bench overlooking the bluff to sit and reflect. I soon realized that this presence was my grandfather.

I had been only four years of age when my grandfather had passed suddenly of a heart attack, yet he has been around me my entire life in another dimension. My grandfather was my supporter, guide, and spiritual cheerleader from across the veil. It seemed that whenever I was going through a major spiritual shift or growth opportunity in my life, my grandfather would make his presence known to me, as if to be supportive and lighten the impact. So I have learned that when he appears, as I mentioned in an earlier chapter, there is a major shift that occurs within me and my existence. It is as if he is part of my initiation team from the other side.

Wanting to confirm who the presence was that was with me, I decided to sit on a nearby bench and enter into meditation. As I sat there, I closed my eyes and asked who was there. The voice returned, "Your grandfather." I immediately felt his presence, and could see him in my mind's eye, a very strong secure energy full of love and compassion. I felt his arm around my shoulder as I sat on the bench. His hands were warm and immensely large, as I remembered from my early childhood. Tears welled up in my eyes; the crying began. He told me that he knew that I was experiencing some challenges in my personal life and indeed I was—starting a new business, half-way through graduate school, and really trying to get clear on who I was as a person. He also informed me that he was there to assist me in getting through them. He said that my life would be more wonderful than I could imagine, and that he was very proud of me.

He then said, "I have someone who wants to see you." Next thing I knew, a woman who resembled my grandmother, Carmella, appeared. At first I did not recognize her; she appeared much younger than I remembered her. She had dark brown long wavy hair, a beautiful complexion, and looked as if she was in her thirties. I then remembered that those who pass onto the next world often appear to those still here in the physical world the way they felt the best when they were alive.

My grandmother said, "Dolores, there have been many things that I have learned since my passing. Many things I did not do so well in my life and that I am not proud of. I am here to ask for your forgiveness, can you forgive me?"

Tears were welling up in my eyes and streaming down my checks uncontrollably. I then responded, "Grandma, can you ever forgive me?"

We embraced energetically and I sensed a huge clearing occurring. Healing can take place between souls even though one person is no longer physically on earth. Our loved ones and friends are still there despite the lack of a physical form. Life is eternal and lessons are learned from the other side as well as here on earth. Growth continues on without form. All are continuously evolving to infinity.

What You Can Do to Have Spiritual Wellness

- Work on forgiveness, most importantly self-forgiveness. We tend to be the hardest on ourselves and treat our friends or strangers better than we treat ourselves.

- Know that just because a person is no longer alive, does not mean that forgiveness cannot occur. Our deceased loved ones are still present and alive without a physical body. They are often reaching out to us for forgiveness as much as we are.

- Work on forgiveness by using the following *Forgiveness Script*. This three-part process addresses forgiving others, asking forgiveness of others, and most importantly forgiving one's self—self-forgiveness.

I forgive _____ for _____ not only in this lifetime, but in all other lifetimes as well, whether it occurred consciously or unconsciously, and if it influenced each of our mental, emotional, physical, and or spiritual bodies.

I ask for forgiveness of _____ for _____ not only in this lifetime, but in all other lifetimes as well, whether it occurred consciously or unconsciously, and if it influenced each of our mental, emotional, physical, and or spiritual bodies.

Most importantly, I forgive myself for _____ to myself___ not only in this lifetime, but in all other lifetimes as well, whether it occurred consciously or unconsciously, and if it influenced my mental, emotional, physical and or spiritual bodies.

Dolores L. Fazzino, DPN, RN

Chapter Seven
Experiences from the Casa

*"For those who believe, no words are necessary.
For those who don't believe, no words are possible."*
St Ignatius

As a student of personal and spiritual growth, I have a curiosity about unique spiritual approaches to healing. I know that more exists than what one can physically see. For me, the dimensions of the unseen are intriguing and awe inspiring. There is so much more that is unseen than one can ever imagine. And that I am blessed and humbled to be given glimpses of those dimensions.

This insight has changed my perspective on healing and about health issues, and about the crises that masses of humanity are currently experiencing. Being trained in western medicine as a nurse practitioner, the allopathic model of healing is primarily focused on the physical aspect, with vague threads of the mental, emotional, and spiritual aspects laced through. But in actuality, the physical, mental, emotional, and spiritual components of our humanness are matrixed together to form a unique and elaborate tapestry. This tapestry is our individual blueprint; each one of us has our own unique pattern that makes up who we are and what we are all about.

As part of my growth and personal healing process, I am constantly exploring, reading, and experiencing different healing modalities. One of the most fascinating modalities that I have found is that of psychic surgery.

There are two distinct types of psychic healing within psychic surgery. The first type is where psychic healers conduct surgical changes in the etheric body (astral double) of the person which results in changes within the physical body. Often times the spirits of dead physicians assist and influence the psychic healer. The observers of the psychic surgery will see the psychic surgeon enter a trance state from which he or she conducts a demonstration of hand motions resembling removing and cutting above the body of the person requesting healing.

George Chapman, a British healer, used of this type of psychic surgery. He claimed that while in trance he would be controlled by the deceased surgeon Dr. Lang. Working through Chapman, Dr Lang would diagnose, lay his hands on the patient, or make movements similar to a phantom operation.

The second type of psychic surgery is where physical demonstrations of actual surgeries are conducted by the psychic surgeon. The psychic surgeons use the physical body of a medium who is in a trance state to conduct physical operation on people. These occur within the spiritualist communities of the Philippines and Brazil. The physical demonstrations of psychic surgery involve incisions made with unsterile surgical instruments, using bare hands, removing the diseased tissue, and causing an instantaneous healing of the incision. All while the medium is in a trance, altered state of consciousness, or even unconscious as Edgar Cayce. The soul of the Medium steps aside and allows his physical body to be used as a vessel for the spirit doctor. The Medium usually has no recall of the events that occurred while their physical body has been borrowed by the psychic surgeon.

Tony Agpaoa in the Philippines and Jose Arigo in Brazil are two examples of famous psychic surgeons that practice this type psychic surgery.

There are other psychic surgeons that practice both etheric and physical demonstrations of psychic surgery. Of those, João Teixeira de Faria, internationally known as John of God or João de Deus, is one of them. His spiritual center, the Casa de Dom Inacio, is located in the beautiful countryside of Abadiania, Goais, Brazil. People travel from all parts of the world to witness and experience the healing energies of the phalange of entities (spirit beings). Many seekers come for healing after western medicine has nothing further to offer them. Many have been healed of ailments for which traditional western medicine has no cure.

Personally, I have witnessed the healing of others as well as my own miraculous healings.

In March, 2008, I decided to reward myself for the completion of my doctoral studies with a trip to visit John of God, in Brazil. I had always been fascinated with psychic surgery, and I felt that this would be an appropriate time for me to explore it, and enhance my spiritual growth. Being a student of life, I felt the urge to go there, as if it were a calling of sorts. Things in my life seemed to be going fairly well, yet I felt as if I was at a standstill in my personal growth.

It seemed that the same patterns or soul lessons kept recurring, but often with another aspect of the pattern which would give me a different perspective of that issue. I wondered how the same things could keep occurring, yet be different. It was as if I was experiencing the movie Ground Hog Day continually over the years. It got to the point that I felt as if I had come to a big wall and did not know how to move through or around it, in order get on with my life. I felt stuck, trapped, and blocked on some level.

The decision to go to Brazil started a sequence of events that seemed to fall into place effortlessly and magically. As we say, once we commit to something, the actual journey begins. Thus, such was the case for me. Once I made the decision to go to Brazil for December 2008, things started lining up effortlessly, as if I was supposed to be going. I am sure others have had similar experiences and for me this was a sign that I was supposed to go there.

I spoke to a colleague of mine about my plans. She then told me that her mother had gone to Brazil to see John of God with a guide, Josie RavenWing. I felt that this was a sign, so I contacted Josie and booked my trip for December with her. A lot transpired as I prepared for my journey to see John of God. As a validation, clients for my healing practice increased, which provided the extra income to pay for my adventure to Brazil. I felt that I was being guided and directed. My connection to gemstones and crystals started to manifest. I found that I was very drawn to crystals, especially those that were from Brazil.

In September, I went to Sedona, and spent time on a vision quest. I felt that this was time that I required to clear and ground myself, in preparation for what I was to experience in Brazil. This trip assisted me in releasing very deep issues around my father. In fact, while I was on this quest, I received word that my father had become very ill, requiring hospitalization, and surgery to release adhesions that had obstructed his abdomen. He fully recovered. I felt that as I cleared my issues with him, he also had cleared his as well.

In anticipation of going to Brazil, I planned to spend a few days visiting my parents in Florida prior to my departure to the Casa in Abadiania. My visit was lovely and I took pictures of them to bring to the Casa for a blessing by John of God.

In the evening, I arrived at the pousada in Abadiania which would be my home for the next two weeks, and was greeted by Josie. Though it was too dark by then to see, I felt the energy within my physical body. It was like a humming or slight buzzing, as if all my cells were waking up. That evening I slept soundly and awoke the next morning well rested.

The next day the rest of the group met up with Josie; we toured the Casa and were oriented in their protocols. The grounds were beautiful, serene, and healing. It felt to me as if an open portal of love from the other side was connected to the Casa. I could feel pure love radiating upon me that caused tears of joy to fall from my eyes. I sensed that it was a bridge between this world and other worlds, one that some of us only get a slight glimpse of periodically. It definitely felt magical. I felt that I had come home.

The following day our group, along with hundreds of other people, attended the morning session. Josie translated my request in Portuguese and John of God, who was in Entity or trance with one of dozens of spiritual doctors and beings, told me, "Surgery this afternoon." I was elated! I was so very excited; I wanted to have that experience and see what it was all about. As I left the Casa to return to my pousada, I felt a sensation in my lower abdomen, back, and both legs, as if I was receiving an anesthetic. The sensation was similar to receiving an epidural block, where the lower body becomes numb or falls asleep.

The afternoon came, and I found myself seated with about one hundred others who would be having surgery that session. We were instructed to close our eyes and focus on the healing that we would like to receive. At that time, we were also asked if there was anyone who wanted to receive a physical demonstration of surgery, if so, to raise his or her hand. Those who chose that option were moved to the general meeting area where these procedures were performed in front of those waiting to see John of God. Prayers were recited such as the Our Father and Hail Mary.

As I sat in meditation, I received my surgical procedure which was done by my own personal team of entities or spiritual doctors and helpers. I felt sensations in my physical body, as well as a flood of emotions that were being removed from my energy field. After thirty minutes, at the end, John of God came into the room and incorporated one of the many entities that work through John of God (at least thirty spiritual doctors, saints, and ascended masters), and announced that our surgeries were complete. We were to then go to the Casa pharmacy, get our post-surgery herbs, return to our pousada and rest for the next twenty- four hours. I found that as I stood up I felt a bit tipsy.

I returned to our pousada, and for the next twenty-four hours remained in bed resting. We were all instructed to stay in bed; as our energy field was now wide open from the surgery we needed to avoid outside energies from entering our field. We were not allowed to read, listen to music, or speak to anyone else for that designated time to allow deeper healing. I felt as if I had received anesthesia and was recovering from the surgery. My meals were brought to me and I only got up out of bed to go to the rest room. I slept most of the time and had some very vivid dreams.

After my day of convalescence, I took a shower and noticed that I had what appeared to be a small one and half inch scar above my left breast and below my clavicle. With further examination I noticed that there seemed to be sutures. I was so excited that I shared this with Josie, our guide. I know that I did not have a physical surgery, yet, whatever occurred in my energy field transferred to my physical body. The scar lasted for about a day and then was gone. The next week, energetically, I felt indeed that I was recovering from a surgical procedure. I would fatigue easily, and could not tolerate being in the sun for long periods of time, which we were told to avoid anyway. I spent that next day, Friday, at the Casa in the current room meditating.

The current rooms are areas in the Casa where one can sit in meditation and receive additional healing as well as be in service to those who are coming to see the entity incorporated in John of God. In the current rooms while one is in meditation, the energy from the other side is transferred through each person who is meditating. This allows healing and spiritual clearings for each of those sitting there and through us to each person waiting in line so that the Entity can better experience each person's true condition. Those who are waiting are often there on an unconscious level as well as a conscious level. When one sits in the current room, one receives energy as well as gives energy. I found it necessary to ground myself energetically to better handle the strong energies that I was experiencing in my body. It was as if I could feel other people's pain. Grounding my energy field assisted me with being able to handle these sensations and release them into the Earth to be transmuted and transformed. My experiences sitting in the current rooms have been among my most profound ones at the Casa.

During my current room experiences, I received visits from my deceased loved ones, in particular, my paternal grandfather, Salvatore, who I mentioned in prior chapters and who had been of great support to me. The first time he came to me in the current room, he smiled at me. I asked him if he was now one of the Casa entities. He said no, but that he liked to come and visit there often. It was nice to connect with him. Next I felt this overwhelming, rather large energetic presence. It pretty much stopped me in my tracks. Though I could not see this energy, I was able to sense and feel the expansiveness of the energy field. I telepathically asked the energetic field who it was. The field replied that his name was Reza. I then asked Reza when his last human incarnation had occurred, to which he immediately responded, 2,500 BC. He then showed himself, as a very tall man, a giant with dark hair and eyes, wearing a beautiful ornate robe. I then asked him if he was an entity of the Casa and he replied yes, and asked me if I wanted to see what occurs spiritually in the surgery room. I said, "Absolutely!"

Considering that I had just experienced having an etheric surgery myself, and with my background as a nurse practitioner assisting in surgery in the States, I was very excited! I always knew that there was more going on in the surgeries that I assisted on, yet never got to see it from the spiritual perspective. While continuing to meditate in the current room, Reza brought me with him to the surgery room at the Casa. I could see a least one hundred people sitting in mediation in the surgery room. Above each person was their etheric field (aura, energy field, etheric double) and around each etheric field there were at least five to six spirit doctors working in tandem in multiple areas of the etheric field. I sat there in awe of what I was witnessing. The visual that was revealed to me—the energy field, which contains the mental, emotional, and spiritual aspects was operated on to remove blocks, or distortions—was assisting with the physical healing as well. I then realized that I was back in the current room meditating. For me, I knew that life had taken a new turn, and I sensed that much more would be revealed in the future.

An additional experience occurred during the trip was that of being a surrogate for my father's psychic surgery. I had brought a picture of my father with me to Brazil to have a blessing. I was informed by John of God that he would benefit by coming to the Casa to have psychic surgery. Knowing that it would be physically challenging for my father to travel from where he lived in Florida to Brazil, I requested permission to be his surrogate for his surgery.

I notified my father and mother of the plans and got my father's permission for me to be the surrogate for his procedure. I gave him the same instructions as if he was physically at the Casa receiving the psychic surgery in person. There was a time difference of two hours from where I was in Abadiania and where my father was located in Florida. I informed my father that at 6 a.m. he was to lay down and rest because the process would be starting in Brazil. I also gave him the same follow up instructions that I had received; it would be necessary that he spend the day in bed resting, no TV, or reading, and only to get up to use the bathroom or to eat.

At the Casa on the day of his procedure, I was in the surgery room at 8 a.m. with the other people who were undergoing surgery. Since I was a surrogate for my father, I had his picture on my lap. I was instructed to close my eyes as the prayers began. I placed my hand on my dad's picture and my other hand over my heart. The next thing I knew was that I was transported to where my father was in his home in Florida along with several other spirit doctors. They asked me to hold and cradle my father's etheric head as they operated within his energy field. I felt such intense emotion that tears were streaming down my face, and I began to sob. I believe that we had been there for no longer than thirty minutes at the most, when the spirit doctors infused a yellow serum in my father's etheric body; we then returned to where I was physically sitting at the Casa in the surgery room. The next thing that I heard was that the surgeries were complete. As I exited the surgery room, I could not stop crying. It was the most profound experience of being in service that I had ever experienced. I am forever humbled. There is indeed more occurring than one can physically see, and I began to sense just how much spirit assistance might be present when I returned to the United States and assisted in future surgeries.

I checked in with my parents the next day. My mother said that my father slept most of the twenty-four hours and was feeling well over all. As time progressed, my father seemed lighter in spirit and his health challenges seemed to dissipate. I learned from the experience that energy and spirit know no distance. And that the healing energy transmitted from a distance can be experienced by the person receiving it.

What You Can Do to Have Spiritual Wellness

- Give yourself permission to follow your intuition or your gut feelings for a day. Let your day be led by your feelings, instead of your thoughts.

- Explore different options for healing and wellness. Many can safely be combined with western medicine and assist the process of healing and wellness.

- Create more balance in your life. Remember to work and to play as well. Include the body, mind, and soul in your life.

- Ignite and live your passion. Create a list of the attributes describing the person you would like to be and become the person that list describes.

- Be of service to others. Volunteering gives you an opportunity to practice random acts of kindness, and to get out of your ego.

Dolores L. Fazzino, DPN, RN

Chapter Eight
Our Pets as Familiars

*"Until one has loved an animal,
a part of one's soul remains unawakened."*
Anatole France

Our animal companions are some of our lifetime companions while we are on our earth journey. They can be our support system, confidants, protectors, and friends. Our pets are here to remind us that we are appreciated and unconditionally loved no matter what we may think or believe about ourselves.

Our pets may also have been with us in prior lifetimes. When that is the case they, too, may choose to reincarnate with our soul group, to support, gain knowledge, and wisdom at their soul's level. Animals are highly evolved and intelligent, but they do not communicate in the same manner as humans, their form of communication is telepathic.

This form of telepathy involves the projecting of pictures, rather than words. For example, if you would like the cat or dog to sit on your lap, project to them a picture of them lying comfortably on your lap. The next thing you know the animal will come to you and do just that.

At times, my cat will project information to me, such as, please check my food bowl, or my litter box needs some cleaning. And on occasion, she gives me messages about where she came from and how we are acquainted from previous lifetimes.

Animals are our helpers and assistants. I call them our familiars. Familiars are animals with whom we have a magical connection. Throughout history, familiars have been given a bad rap, so to speak. They were associated with witchcraft, evil, and other forms of malevolence.

However, today animals or our familiars are those who have a strong psychic and emotional bond with their human. They assist and witness our life events with us, and remind us that, "I am there for you. You are not alone." They may come into our lives in the most unusual ways.

Our cherished pets and familiars pick us out. It really is not the other way around. They may be a stray that continues to cross paths with us, like coming to our door, or following us home one day. Or if we go to the pet store, shelter, or breeder, they follow us around or come to us and want to be held. With every pet in my life, the animal always came to me. When I picked it up, it would climb up my left arm and sit on my shoulder. For me it was a sign that it was mine!

Our pets can also assist in the healing work for others as well as ourselves. Animals have amazing healing powers. As a healer, my cat loves to participate in sessions with clients. She will be present in the room or even on the client for the session, as long as the client does not have an allergy to cats. I call her my personal "Cat Scanner" since she seems to go to where the physical issue is and lies there to offer assistance.

When we meditate, the animals often do so as well. They come and gather round the meditating person, and sit in the energy that is being created by the mediation. It is as if they are participating in the experience.

Our pets are our protectors. Animals are also sensitive to energies, which are attached to the physical being as well as the spiritual being. They are so tuned in to energy that they are aware when there is danger or something unusual is happening. Have you ever witnessed a pet leave the room or hiss or growl at a person, or even stare and not come near the person? Take heed, for this is a warning that the person may not be who they appear to be and that an ongoing connection with that particular person may not be healthy. This behavior may also occur when the person is carrying a multitude of beings or entities in their energy field, baggage of the spiritual kind. And of course, this also can occur when there are spirits in the environment as well.

Animals can come back to us lifetime after lifetime, not only once or twice but numerous times in one lifetime. Allow me to share a story to illustrate this.

It was a very sad day, a day that I knew that I would have to experience sooner or later. I t was the day that I had to put down my beloved Jasmine. Jasmine was my Tortie (tortoise-shell cat), Siamese, blue-eyed cat; she was eleven years old and was my familiar. Jasmine had developed an over-active thyroid which had not responded to conventional veterinary medical treatment.

I adopted Jasmine as a two-month-old kitten. She was one of a litter of six kittens that were in a pet store. Out of the six kittens, she came right up to me, climbed up my body and sat on my left shoulder. I instantly knew that she was mine, and adopted her. I asked her what she wanted to be called. She projected Jasmine. She joined me and Pogey, my two-year-old Burmese-mix male cat. It was he who encouraged me to go and adopt another cat. Pogey was lonely. I was working long hours and when I would get home he would bring all his cat toys to my feet and then tap my leg and want me to toss and play with him. I asked him if he wanted a companion, and he responded, "Meow," so I said to him that I would find him one.

There was something very special about Jasmine. She was sweet, loveable, and very much attuned to her environment. Throughout her life, she was my support, companion, helper, and assistant in the energy healing sessions that I conducted. I felt an extremely strong bond with her, as if she had been with me in numerous past lifetimes.

Putting her down was one of the most difficult things that I ever had to do. That day in October 2009, my friend Deb DeLisi came with me to the veterinarian's office. As we put her down, both Deb and I were sobbing. She piped up and asked, "Why is it that we sometimes cry more for our animals than our family members when they pass?" Both of us just started laughing, for that was just so true! Maybe it is because they just love us for who we are without any judgment. As Jasmine was being put to sleep, I told her that she would always be welcome in my home and to come back to me in a new healthy form. As her heart stopped, I felt a string remove itself from my heart, and an immense peace and joy. I saw her spirit in the upper corner of the exam room at the vet's office.

The next day prior to getting out of bed, and opening my eyes, I saw my Jasmine right in front of my face. It really scared and startled me at first, for I knew that she was not alive, yet on the spirit level she was very much there.

Our Pets as Familiars

For several months I contemplated getting another cat. Jasmine's companion cat Boo, did not seem to miss her and loved getting all the attention from me. Then in May of 2010, while meditating, Jasmine came to me, she said that she was coming back. I said to her, "Great." I then did not give it much more thought. However, the next month at the end of June, she came to me again while I was in meditation. She told me that she was here and to come look for her at the end of August. That nearly blew me out of the water. She also told me that she would look very similar to what she looked like when she was last here, as she liked being regal looking and in a Siamese body and wanted to be female again.

So at the end of August, I started looking for her. I looked on line, at shelters, and at pet stores. It seemed I kept meeting obstacle upon obstacle to reconnect with my familiar. In fact, one place told me before I could even see an animal that I had to complete an application and go through an involved process. I responded to her, "It is not us who picks out the pet; it is the pet that chooses us. So why can't I see the animal, and then if it is the correct one, then complete the paper work?" I did not et the response from her that I hoped for!

Out of frustration, I spoke with some friends, who suggested going to Craig's List on the internet. Sure enough there was a listing for a litter of six kittens in Carlsbad, a Siamese mix as well. I called and spoke with the owner and made an appointment to see them. On the way to see the kittens, I telepathically asked the kitten, "What do you want to be called?" Immediately, I heard, "Meeka."

When I arrived, I met the litter of kittens, and the one that came to me and sat on my left shoulder was the spirit I was seeking. She was about two months old; very blue eyes, chocolate points, and Siamese.

71

I had found my old friend!

When we arrived home, Boo my other cat, met us at the door. This was unusual because Boo never meets anyone at the door. Then Meeka started running around the house as if she owned it! Several other familiar idiosyncrasies occurred over the next several months.

When clients would come to my home office for sessions, Meeka would sleep under the massage table. Jasmine used to be very involved with the healing sessions, usually being in the room, sitting on the area of the client that required healing.

Another thing that started happening was that Meeka would climb into the shower after I was done, sit in the water and start to groom herself. This was a trait of Jasmine's. I thought, very interesting.

And lastly, in November of 2010, while I was sitting in meditation , Jasmine came to me and her face morphed into Meeka's face. At that point I knew that Meeka was indeed my beloved Jasmine. From that time on, Meeka started conveying a lot of information to me telepathically. She also projected a picture from my childhood, when she was another cat that I had. She said that she also was my Momma Kitty, that cat that I had as a teenager. Meeka also wanted me know that she will be coming back in her next lifetime as a human. I asked her if I would be her mother in that lifetime. She let me know that it was not determined as of yet. She said that she had come back to me numerous times so that I could teach her what it was like to be human.

What You Can Do to Have Spiritual Wellness

- Spend time with your pets. Animals teach us a lot about behavior and life. And they too have emotions and feelings.

- Adopt a pet from a shelter. These animals are in need of good homes and will show you a lifetime of joy and love.

- Volunteer at a pet shelter if you are unable to have a pet. Being of service to our animal companions enriches our lives.

Dolores L. Fazzino, DPN, RN

Chapter Nine
A Celebration of My Mother's Transition

Those we love don't go away, they walk beside us every day.
Unseen, unheard, but always near; still loved, still missed and very dear.
Anonymous

Spirits communicate with us through a wide variety of modalities. Orbs are one such way. Orbs are vessels in which the spirit comes to let us know that it is present. For some, they are evident and are able to be seen through our physical eyes as well as our psychic eyes. They appear in pictures, sometimes as blurs, spots, waves, in multiple colors. I believe they occur in pictures to remind us that we are not alone and that the spirit world is still very connected to each of us. Often times they are found in nature, especially in areas that are highly spiritually attuned to the nature deities, elementals, and in highly energized natural formations and vortexes.

Vortexes are transition points where the energy shifts from one dimension to another dimension. These are also openings or portals that allow spirits to move from this world to the next. Portals are often found in many holy or sacred places, and can be sensed by people with their intuitive and psychic abilities, as well as seen in digital photos.

I believe that orbs are gifts for those who are ready to receive them. They are messengers and bring information to assist those who capture them in photos as well as for any people who are in a photograph with one or more orbs. Often in meditation, a photo showing orbs brings a lot of information that can be received through your higher self. The information is a gift, a validation that we are more connected to the other side than we might have imagined. It is as if these spirits in the orbs are here to give us support, encouragement, and hope that we are not alone on our journey. They are reminders that they are ever present with us on our paths, even when we may feel alone, abandoned, and alienated.

If you look closely, sometimes faces appear within the orbs. As I mentioned earlier, these are the vehicles in which some spirits travel to our Earth realm.

Other vehicles of transport are ectoplasm, which is a vaporous-like material that is created by a physical medium that is in trance state and is calling an entity into spiritual contact from the other side. This ectoplasm emerges most often through the orifices of the medium's body, including the mouth, nose, eyes, and ears, as well as through the hands. The spirit then uses the ectoplasm to have a visible form through which they can then interact in our physical universe. Ectoplasm can be captured on digital camera, at anytime during the day in the early evening, dusk or dawn or other times when natural light is present, Ectoplasm can best be seen in the dark by the naked eye. Like the orbs, these spirits can then bring messages, and the awareness that we are not alone on our journey.

I want to share the personal story of my mother's passing. It was an uncanny event for me. So much had transpired by this point in my journey, I felt as if I was on a roll. Have you ever had the experience that things were occurring in your life that made no logical sense, and yet, when you followed your intuition, amazing things unfolded?

In May of 2010, I was employed in corporate America. I had been previously self-employed for sixteen years; but with the direction the economy had taken, I opted for more financial stability and took a job at a local hospital. Believe me, I went kicking and screaming, yet I knew that I also had certain things I wanted to accomplish. These included refinancing my home, having health insurance, and paying down a very large financial debt that I had created for myself.

I started the job as a supervisor in the operating room at a small hospital. But nearly a year later in April of 2011, I was not feeling fulfilled by my current job. I was constantly exhausted, unappreciated, and extremely stressed out. As my spiritual practice, I would meditate daily chanting Nam Myo Renge Kyo. I prayed to God, asking him to point me in the direction that I needed for my career. I said that I would go anywhere in the world to be of service to both God and humanity.

My prayers were answered on May 1, 2011. Out of the blue, I received an email from a friend, Josie RavenWing. She had been my guide in December of 2008 when I had gone to Brazil to visit the Casa and John of God. Under her guidance and leadership, my experience at the Casa was transformational, expansive, humbling, and profound. Josie and I continued to correspond over the years. In her email she inquired if I would be interested in coming to Brazil as her assistant to work with a large group that she would be overseeing at the Casa June 6 through 18, only a month away. Of course my response was, "Absolutely!" I knew that no matter what transpired with my job, I was being led to go to Brazil to be of service.

I asked my interim director if I could take time off and after several days she denied my request. She said that I would have to make a decision. I had already made that decision in the event of this circumstance, and said thank you to her. I decided since I was not valued as an employee there that I would give a two-week notice and proceed with my plans. Since I had at least four more weeks left before my June 4 departure to Brazil, my enthusiasm was elevated!

The interim director and I had not really bonded. I felt she used me as a scapegoat, and was doing her best to eliminate me from the department. In fact, about two and half weeks prior to my departure to Brazil, she called me into her office to put me on probation with a written disciplinary action. I suspected that she'd had it in for me since the beginning. She said that I had issues with people and was not management material, not a leader. She told me I had a month to get my act together, or I would be out of a job. Of course, she neither asked my side of what was going on nor for my input. I was extremely calm, for I knew that she was projecting all of her inadequacies on to me. I asked if this information would be in my employee file, she said yes. I said, if I chose to resign, would this be deleted from my file, and she said yes. So I told her that my last day would be June 3.

All the signs were there that this was what I was supposed to do. Once I made my choices and decisions, I felt a tremendous release and freedom. It was as if the angels around me were supporting me and handing me my diploma; I graduated! It was no longer my responsibility to accept being unappreciated nor to compensate for others' issues.

Little did I know what was really occurring on an unseen level and what was about to unfold over the next several weeks. My parents, who were retired and living in Florida, had been starting to have health challenges. Since my Brazilian opportunity had presented itself, my mother had fallen quite ill.

Things had been out of sorts with my mom since the end of Feb of that year. She had been chasing a palmetto bug around the kitchen, went to step on the bug, lost her balance and fell to the ground. This particular event was the beginning of some health issues that my mother manifested for herself.

Unfortunately, Mom had shattered her right wrist and had fractured her back. Two weeks later she had surgery to repair her wrist and was fitted for an external back brace. She was on pain pills that upset her stomach. I believed that she was getting an ulcer due to the amount of stress that she was under, not only with her health, but also worrying about my father.

My mother was my father's care taker. I believe that she felt that no one else could take care of him as well as she could. Over the next few months, my mom seemed to have more issues with her stomach, lots of pain, and even blood in her stool. She went to the gastroenterologist, and underwent tests and studies. The results were that she did indeed have a peptic ulcer. She was placed on medication for that issue, but it made her feel even worse. She had no appetite, was nauseated, and did not feel at all well. Her symptoms continued.

On May 10, my mom felt as if there was an obstruction under her rib cage. When she ate, she felt that the food could not go down. My father brought her to the emergency department at the local hospital. They admitted her, performed a CAT scan, and did an endoscopy procedure. In the back of my mind, I prayed that she did not have pancreatic cancer. As a nurse practitioner, sometimes one knows too much. I was relieved to know that her CT scan came back normal, no tumors or abnormal findings. The endoscopy results indicated a diagnosis of peptic ulcer disease and she was obstructed due to a high level of inflammation. The plan was to keep her on nutrition intravenously in order give the intestine and stomach a break and to allow for a reduction in swelling in the area.

My mom began to talk about not being around much longer and that if she had any surgery she probably would not survive. I was taken aback, because this was very out of character for my mother to talk like this. Her attitude definitely got my attention.

As a healer, I provided my services to my mother. Distant healing was effective, she could feel the energy despite the three thousand-mile distance from myself to her. What I found most interesting and rather puzzling, was that every time I worked with my mother, I could see the brightest white light that I have ever experienced. It was in the hospital. I felt that it was a sign that everything was going to be alright. I felt that my mom had a lot of life force in her body and was going to survive. I assumed this to be so, but it was not the case. In retrospect, I believe that the radiant white light was the other side calling for her to come home. I did not realize this until after events of the next ten days had occurred.

The information that I received from the spirit doctors for my mother were issues around forgiveness. I spoke with my mother about this. I was mindful of how I approached the topic with her, for in the past there had been much denial and resistance when forgiveness was discussed. I explained that sometimes we hold grudges in our lives that we are conscious about. But the ones we try to block from consciousness, are the ones that most need to be forgiven and released.

I asked my mom if she would be open to working on that. Much to my surprise, she was. I explained to her how to do the process. I told her it was not necessary to relive the experience, or try to remember something that is unconscious. Before you go to sleep, ask God to assist you in forgiveness, including those things that you remember, and particularly those things that you do not remember. Practice forgiveness for things that you did to others, forgiveness for the things that others have done to you, and most importantly, forgiveness for yourself.

I checked in with her a couple of days later, and she said that she has been working on forgiveness. I told her that was excellent, and to keep doing so.

After about a week, my mom was restarted on liquids and then solid food. She was ready to be discharged when she felt ill again and began to vomit. The staff admitted her to the rehab unit, which was a huge mistake, because the doctors who were working with her did not know that she was still in the hospital and did not see her. After about a week, (this took place over Memorial Day weekend), her gastroenterologist was contacted and my mother was transferred to another hospital. She arrived there, was seen by a surgeon, worked up for surgery, and had surgery on June 3.

Prior to her surgery I gave my mom guided imagery to assist her with experience in surgery. I felt that this allowed my mother to relax. At the end of our session, I told her that I loved her and that no matter what happened that she would be safe. I went into meditation and blessed the surgical suite for her surgery. Once again, there was so much white light coming from the surgical suite that it was peaceful and serene.

After Mom's surgery, the surgeon shared the findings. He said that Mom had a large tumor in her pancreas, that it was inoperable, involved in the stomach, small intestine, and other vital organs. They were able to bypass the area, so that she would be able to eat. My mother was diagnosed with inoperable pancreatic cancer.

I received the news and was shocked. How could this be? The CT scan showed no tumors, yet somehow there was a very large mass. The next day I was leaving to go to Brazil to assist Josie at the Casa. I knew in my heart of hearts that I was meant to be in Brazil at this time, and I knew that I must proceed with my plans. My decision did not sit well with some immediate family members, but I maneuvered around the family obstacles and emotions.

Knowing the diagnosis and prognosis of my Mom's state of health, I encouraged my family to support whatever she wanted. As a nurse practitioner, I was aware that pancreatic cancer had a low chance of survival and it can end badly. What I truly wished for my mother was to have a good death experience, to go easily, effortlessly and with grace.

I was in contact with my mother on Saturday, June 4 while I was at the Miami airport in route to Brazil. She was still recovering from her anesthetic and surgical procedure. She asked me if there were dark entities on the roof of the hospital. My family thought that she was hallucinating from the pain medication. I knew that she was truly seeing what I have witnessed in my thirty-year history of working in hospitals. Yes, there are dark entities that await the departing souls. They are spirits who have passed and have not crossed over completely to the white light or other side. I call it a purgatory of sorts.

They gain entrance into patients who are sick and thus weak, and die able to feed off some of their energy. In my Mom's case, her clairvoyant sight was opening up and she was able to see this. I explained to her that she was safe and surrounded by the strongest light of protection. My sister also mentioned to me that on Sunday, Mom told her that there was a black man behind her bed with holy water in a bowl.

I arrived in Brazil on Sunday, June 5, got settled in and went to meditate at the Casa. I was warmly greeted by the entities of the Casa. It felt good to be back to a place that I consider my spiritual home.

The next day, Monday, I spoke briefly with my mother. Later that night I was journaling and automatically started to write a poem for her. The words flowed easily. I put the poem aside, not knowing that this was an important aspect of the next sequence of events to unfold.

That night as I was getting ready to sleep, every time I would close my eyes, the brightest white light was in my clairvoyant sight. I usually am a very sound sleeper and drift off to sleep rapidly. After several hours of this experience, I finally settled into sleep. I was not sure what that was all about.

The next day Tuesday, my mom's surgeon delivered the final pathology report. My parents and sister were there when the news was delivered. My mom decided that she did not want anything further done. I spoke to her and supported her wishes, and told her that whatever she decided I would support her no matter what. My family also honored her wishes.

That night, when I went to bed, again, the bright white light was present as I closed my eyes to sleep. And this time, I was having cramps in both my legs. I never get cramps in my legs. It reminded me of my maternal grandmother. Prior to my grandmother passing, she would wake up in the middle of the night, screaming in pain because her legs had cramped up. I would get up and massage them for her. I now believed it was her who was trying to get my attention. So I went into meditation, and in fact it was my grandmother.

The next morning when I awoke, there was a text message from my sister. She said that Mom was transferred to the intensive care unit overnight. I called my sister, she said that Mom was on life support and that she was unconscious. I asked her what had happened. She said that Mom got up to go the bathroom and fell about 11 p.m. The nurse got her back into bed. During the night she suffered a cardiac arrest.

Knowing that my mother was dying, I asked my sister to put the phone up to her ear. My sister insisted that said she couldn't hear me, being unconscious. I told her that she could hear me, and to please put the phone up to her ear. She did, I said good bye to her, and I thanked her for being my mother, my mentor, my friend, and support system. Then I remembered the poem that I'd written on Monday. I read the poem to her:

Dear Mom,
Rest in the white light of peace
Bathe your soul and be reborn
You are loved more than you can ever imagine
You are an eternal being of light, hope and inspiration
It is your choice and you are supported
We love you and are grateful to have your beautiful spirit amongst us
You are carefree, hopeful and rested.

And know that healing occurs on many different levels as well as on the physical
Know that I have loved you before,
I love you now,
And will love you forever,
For love knows no boundaries and knows no distance.
Be at peace and have eternal happiness.
Amen

I then realized that I wrote this poem to assist my mom to cross over.

Being at the Casa to see John of God was probably the best place for me to be for this experience. Later that afternoon, I sat in the current room at the Casa. While there in meditation, I experienced my mother, who was making her transition. My mother always wanted to come to Brazil, and there she was with me in the current room! We had both shared an interest in paranormal and the unseen realms of things. I believe that brought us closer and was a bonding force in our relationship.

Suddenly in my meditation, I was with her, and we were on the other side. There in front of us and extending into the far distance were people lined up three and four abreast. The first person who greeted us was my maternal grandmother, who was my favorite grandmother. She and I were very close in her physical life, and even closer once she passed away in 1977. The next person that greeted us was my mother's Aunt Ann. Aunt Ann was my mother's favorite aunt and she passed away in 1985. The next person that I saw was my paternal grandfather. My grandfather was smiling from ear to ear, he was so happy to see us. It was like a huge party to welcome my mom home to heaven. It was the most amazing experience. There was so much happiness and joy. I sensed that everyone who my mother had known in her life that had predeceased her were there to welcome her.

The next thing I knew I was back in the current room and it was 3:30 p.m. I found out later that evening that my mother passed away at that same time in Florida.

I shared this information with my dad and siblings. My father said that my mom was his father's favorite daughter-in-law, which is probably why he was one of the first people to greet her on the other side. After this experience, I know that love continues no matter what, and that life continues in other realms.

On June 15, a week after my Mom's passing, I was having a crystal bed session at the Casa. During my session, my Mom came to me and was sitting on the massage table. She wanted to let me know that she was doing well and wanted to thank me for helping her cross over. I said that it was my pleasure.

That evening, I decided to take my camera to take some pictures of the Casa at night. At night orbs have a tendency to appear in the pictures. I took several. The best part was downloading them onto the computer and seeing what appeared. That night, there were numerous orbs in all different colors. I also noted that there was a strange phenomenon in several pictures; it was if there was a column with orbs in a vortex formation with something that resembled the planet Saturn. I then realized that this was probably not Saturn, but possibly a space craft of some sort. Puzzled by this, I decided to go out over the next five evenings and see if the same thing was there in the same spot. And sure enough, it was there each and every time, directly about an outdoor bust of St. Ignatius, patron of the Casa. I believe I was seeing the Vortex and possibly a portal where the entities enter through and leave the Casa.

Not sure how to handle this information, I asked Josie to look at the pictures. She told me in all her years of coming to the Casa, she had not seen this before. She suggested that we bring a copy to the Entity (the spirit incorporated in John of God) for more information. We brought him the copy of the photo of the vortex or portal with the unusual craft, and Josie pointed to it and said, "Look, a UFO over the Casa." He looked at it and nonchalantly said, "I know," and had us move on. Josie and I thought that was an interesting response. Josie said that many Brazilians who have attended the Casa over the year have calmly acknowledged the presence of UFOs in the area, so apparently it was no big news to the Entity!

I returned to the States on June 20 to attend my mother's funeral, which was held on June 24. The funeral was beautiful and I was honored and humbled to give the eulogy for my mother.

A month or so passed, and I headed to Florida to spend some time with my father to support him and assist him in going through my mother's belongings. As I said, my mom and I shared a common interest in metaphysics. I felt that in her I'd found a soul sister to share information with. She, too, would read a lot about various aspects of that topic. When I was going through her books, I came across a book on orbs. I never knew she had this, but the timing of finding it so soon after my Casa orb experiences and her transition was startling. I felt somehow like she'd sent me a gift from the other side. I looked forward to continuing our eternal connection. Thanks Mom!

What You Can Do to Have Spiritual Wellness

- Notice what else appears in your photos and environment. Spirits maybe letting you know that they are around.

- Ask for the orbs to appear in your photos when you take picture.

- Know that your connection with your loved ones continues to grow even stronger from the other side. Love like energy knows no boundaries, distance, or time.

- Talk to your deceased loved ones as if they were physically present in the room with you, for they are very much with you. It is as if they stepped through an invisible doorway to the other side.

- If you suddenly think of them out of the blue, know that they too are thinking of you as well.

- Ask them for help, they are more than willing to assist you. Pay attention to the synchronicities that occur.

- Realize that you are never alone and never have been.

Epilogue

Since I have written this book my father, Joseph P. Fazzino, made his transition on December 8, 2013, exactly eighteen months after my mother Frances B. Fazzino. I was blessed to have chosen my parents for this lifetime. I have learned and benefited from the lessons and experiences that were offered to me. These experiences have laid the foundation of who I am in this lifetime and prepared me for what should come in my future years.

I learned more from my father the last eighteen months of his life, than I did in all the previous years. When our mother, his wife passed, the family witnessed a man who transformed himself to be as independent as he could be. I personally learned more about my father's true character at this time. He was brave, sensitive, vulnerable, funny, generous, and very wise. My dad was a tease and had an awesome sense of humor and continued to keep that until the very last days of his life, something I will treasure.

On the day that he passed, I was on my way to work. As I walked toward the front of my hospital building, a beautiful white down feather floated down to ground in front of me, I knew that it was a sign from Dad and that he was ok.

I would like to share a poem by David Romano:

Dolores L. Fazzino, DPN, RN

When Tomorrow Starts without Me

When tomorrow starts without me,
And I am not there to see
If the sun should rise and find your eyes
All filled with tears for me;
I wish so much you wouldn't cry
The way you did today,
While thinking of the many things,
We didn't get to say.
I know how much you love me,
As much as I love you,
And each time you think of me,
I know you'll miss me too;
But when tomorrow starts without me,
Please try to understand,
That an angel came and called my name,
And took me by the hand,
And said my place was ready,
In heaven far about,
And that I'd have to leave behind
All those I dearly love.
But as I turned to walk away,
A tear fell from my eye
For all my life, I'd always thought,
I did not want to die.
I had so much to live for,
So much left yet to do,
It seemed almost impossible,
That I was leaving you.

Epilogue

I thought of all the yesterdays,
The good ones and the bad,
The thought of all the love we shared,
And all the fun we had.
If I could relive yesterday
Just even for a while,
I'd say good bye and kiss you
And maybe see you smile.
But then I fully realized
That this could never be,
For emptiness and memories,
Would take the place of me.
And when I thought of worldly things
I might miss come tomorrow,
I thought of you and when I did
My heart was filled with sorrow.
But when I walked through heaven's gates
I felt so much at home
When God looked down and smiled at me,
From His great golden throne,
He said, "This is eternity, and all I've promised you.
Today your life on earth is past,
But here it starts anew.
I promise no tomorrow,
But today will always last,
And since each day's the same way,
There's no longing for the past
You have been so faithful, so trusting so true.
Though there were times

You did some things
You knew you shouldn't do.
But you were forgiven
And now at last you're free.
So won't you come and take my hand
And share my life with me?"
So when tomorrow starts without me,
Don't think we're far apart,
For every time you think of me,
I'm right here, in your heart.

As I close, my father's passing is truly the best Christmas gift I could receive, knowing that he is at peace and with my mother Frances. I love you, Dad.

Illustrations

Dolores L. Fazzino, DPN, RN

St. Ignatius de Loyola (DomInacio de Loyola).

Closed portal over Casa de Dom Inacio.

Orbs lining the portal above the Casa.

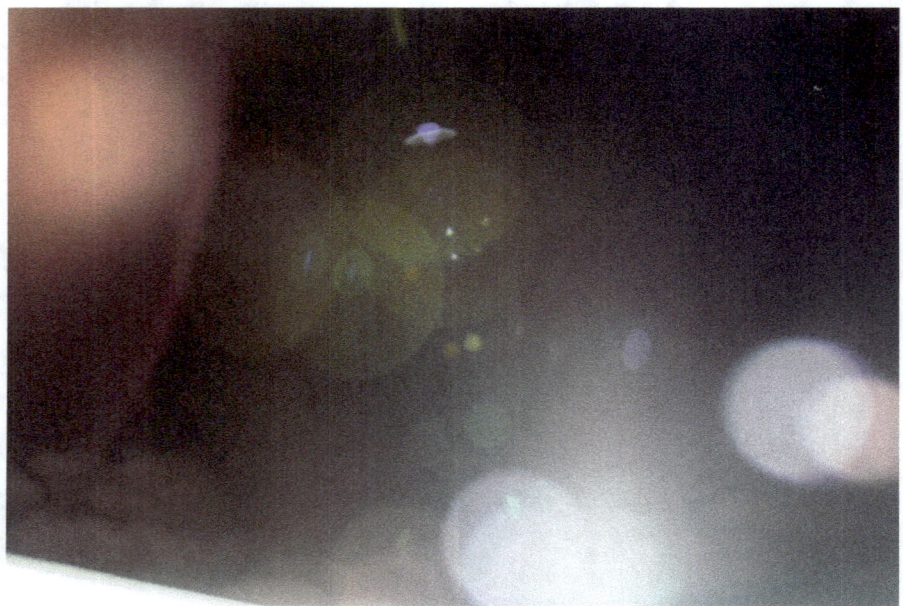

Illustrations

Double spaceships on the external closed portal.

Extoplasm and energy from the bust of Dom Inacio de Loyola at the Casa.

Bust of Dom Inacio de Loyola (St. Ignatius of Loyola) with orbs.

Illustrations

Orb activity above the Casa.

Orbs at the Casa Gardens.

Dolores L. Fazzino, DPN, RN

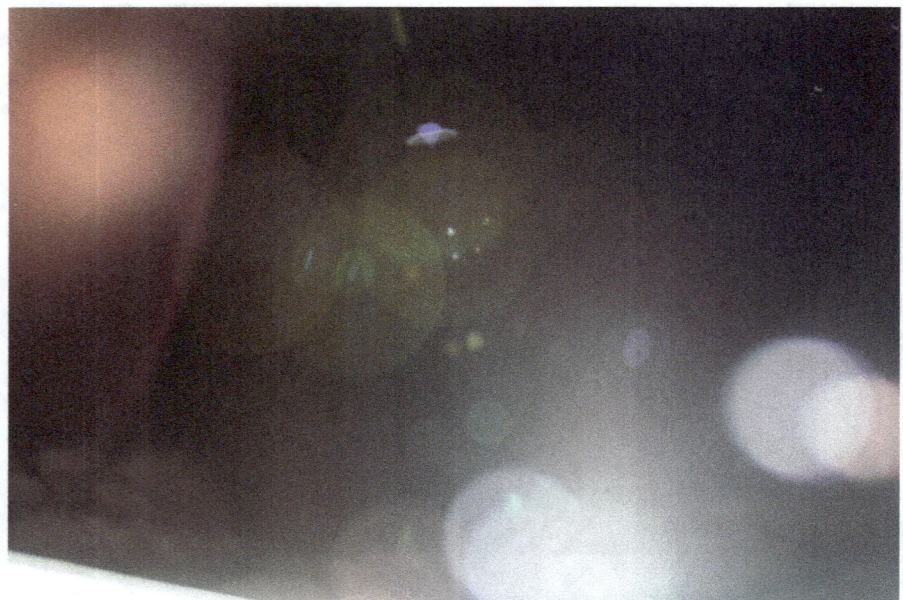

Orbs and portal above the Casa.

Ectoplasm forming near Casa.

Illustrations

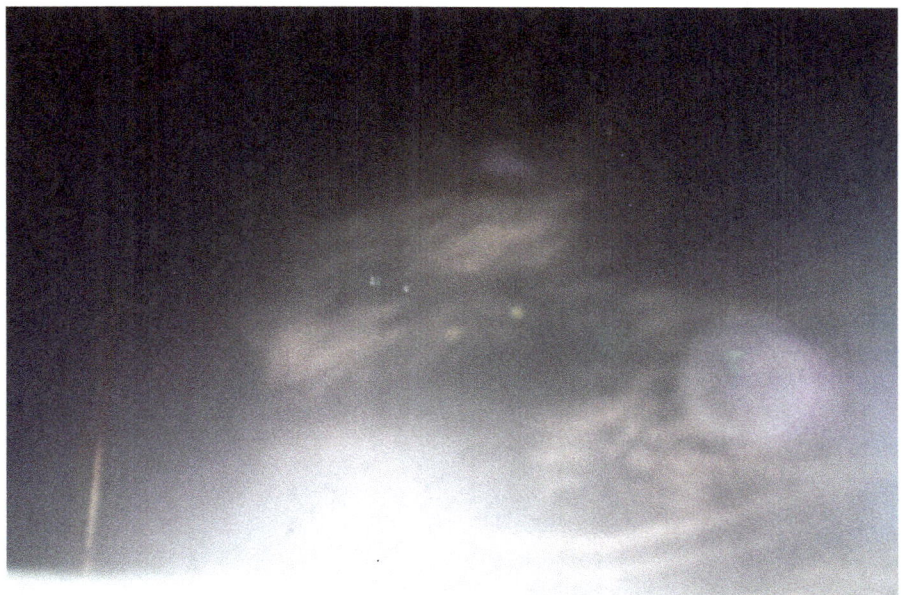

Ectoplasm and orbs at Casa.

Orbs and formation of ectoplasm.

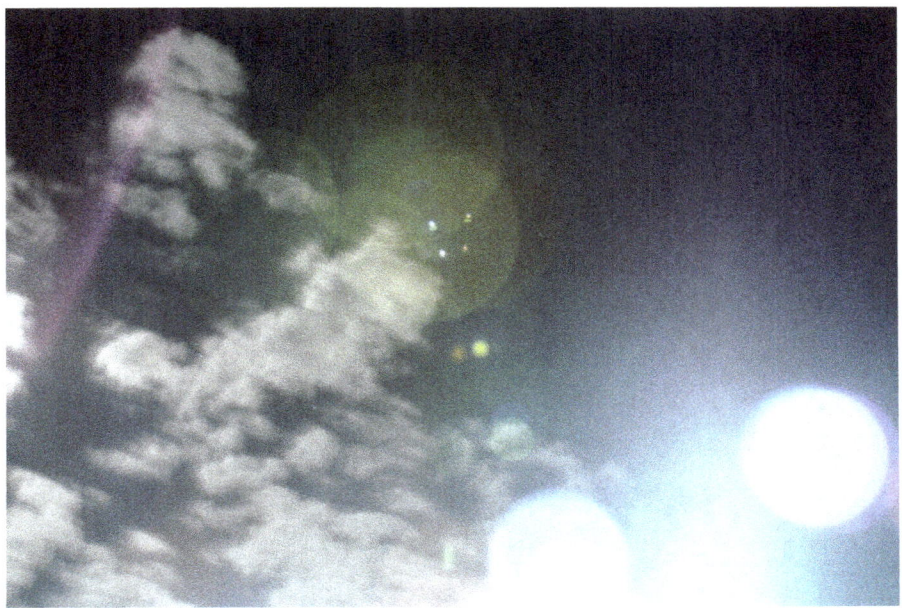

Dolores L. Fazzino, DPN, RN

Above and below: Ectoplasm with full moon June 2011: notice the angel or being forming.

About the Author

Dr. Dolores L. Fazzino, DNP, RN
Wellness Consultant, Professional Speaker, and Author

Dr. Dolores Fazzino, Doctorate of Nursing Practice (DNP), is a Nurse Practitioner, and President of Spiritual Wellness for Life, as well as an international speaker, featured media personality, and author.

With over 35 years of experience working in healthcare, Dolores is the leading authority and expert in combining traditional medicine, energy healing, and spirituality to assist clients move through the emotional, spiritual, and mental, as well as physical life challenges of life with grace and ease. By practicing and training in two worlds, Dolores bridges the physical with spiritual as a Wellness Consultant.

A life-long student of traditional and energy medicine, Dr. Fazzino believes that for a complete healing to occur, the mental, emotional, and spiritual aspects contributing to the issues that created the physical symptoms need to be addressed, in addition to physical symptoms that one is having. She has witnessed reoccurrences of the physical issues, when these areas are not addressed and handled.

Her company, **Spiritual Wellness for Life**, bridges spirituality with physical health. She practices and trains in two worlds: the physical and spiritual. Dolores believes that Spirituality is the glue that holds the body, mind, and soul together.

As a gifted energy healer, Dr. Fazzino assists with the "spiritual interventions or surgeries" that are occurring in our energy fields while she is in session with her clients. The work is similar to the work that she does as an assistant in surgery in the physical world, however it is done while in meditation and trance without physically connecting with the client. Her work connects the physical energy with the energies of the spirit world.

The process assists in removing energetic blocks from one's energy field which allow shifts to occur in the mental, emotional, spiritual and physical bodies. Many have been assisted on their healing paths with this technique. These include those with chronic and terminal illnesses, as well as those who feels stuck in their life and want to make changes.

Dr. Fazzino received her Doctorate in Nursing Practice (DNP) from Case Western Reserve University in 2008. The focus of her doctoral studies included spirituality, spiritual well-being, and energy medicine in preparing patients for surgery. As a life-long student and explorer of healing and spirituality, she travels to Peru and Brazil to experience nontraditional healing methods on a regular basis.

Her first book, *"Spiritual Wellness for Life: Inspirational Life Stories of Forgiveness, Transition, and Healing"* offers spiritual hope and inspiration to others and guidance to attain spiritual wellness, is available on Amazon.com or at www.info-Integrity.com.

She is in private practice as a Wellness Consultant in Encinitas, California, USA. Find out more about Dolores at www.SpiritualWellnessForLife.com

https://www.facebook.com/dolores.fazzino

http://www.linkedin.com/in/doloresfazzino

www.ingramcontent.com/pod-product-compliance
Lightning Source LLC
Chambersburg PA
CBHW052211090526
44584CB00019BA/3046